The Pleasures of Cocaine

The Pleasures of Cocaine

If you enjoy the pleasures of cocaine, this book can save your life.

by Adam Gottlieb

Illustrated by Larry Todd

20TH CENTURY ALCHEMIST

RONIN
Berkeley, CA
www.roninpub.com

The Pleasures of Cocaine

ISBN 0-914171-81-X
ISBN: 9780914171812 - pbook
ISBN: 9781579511272 - ebook
Copyright: 1976 20th Century Alchemist

Published by
RONIN Publishing, Inc.
PO Box 3436
Oakland, CA 94609
www.roninpub.com
Previously published by High Times/Level Press

Credits:
Cover photo art direction: Carlene Schnabel
Cover photographer: Harlan Ang
Cover design: Bonnie Smetts
Paste-up: Hope Emerson Winslow
Typesetting: Aardvark Type

Distributed to the trade by Publishers Group West/Perseus
Printed in the United States of America

TABLE OF CONTENTS

Introduction 7

Enjoying Cocaine Without Abusing It 21

The Pleasures of Cocaine 33

Method of Use 40

Selection of Quality 61

Purification of Cocaine 112

Cultivaiton of Coca 133

Buying and Dealing 146

INTRODUCTORY STATEMENTS ON THIS BOOK AND THE AUTHOR'S ATTITUDE TOWARDS COCAINE USE

It is the personal political philosophy of the author that the adult individual has a biological birthright which allows him (or her) the freedom to be sovereign of his own mind and body and that he may do with himself anything that he pleases as long as this does not directly infringe upon the rights of others. To the author this right appears ethically obvious. If you don't own your own body, then who does? Legally and judicially the guarantee of this right should be implicit in the wordings of the First and Ninth Amendments of the Constitution of the United States of America. If these are not sufficient to spell out this guarantee with absolute certainty, the United States Congress has a moral obligation to create a new Amendment stating that the individual is sovereign of himself in all private matters. The attitude of the American public is definitely taking strides in the directions of favoring this belief. This is reflected in the changes in abortion laws (woman's ownership of her body), in the loosening of laws and taboos regarding personal sexual practices, in the recent judicial consideration of a terminal patient's right to die, and to some extent in the lightening of marijuana use penalties. Properly interpreted and applied, the right

of personal sovereignty should include the right
to take into one's body any substance one desires,
whether it be for nutritional, medicinal, psychedelic
or hedonistic purposes. At present, however, the general awareness of this vaguely understood concept of
freedom has not evolved to a point where it would
include the right to use any drug the individual
chooses. In time we may fully gain the right to be
masters and mistresses of our own minds and bodies.
But we must bear in mind that without knowledge and
good judgment to direct it, freedom will most likely
lead to chaos.

At the time of this writing cocaine is illegal in most
nations including the United States. Still, more and
more people are using it and discovering its pleasures
and usefulness. But cocaine is a double-edged sword.
Although the myth of its "terrible addictiveness" has
been thoroughly disproved, cocaine, like alcohol,
does have its potential for abuse and misuse. Harm
may occur from overdose, prolonged excessive use,
allergic sensitivity (rare), and from some of the adulterants that are combined with it by black market
dealers. The purpose of this book is to convey to the
reader knowledge of both edges of the sword. It contains chapters explaining how to get the most pleasure
out of cocaine and others telling how to avoid its
dangers. In doing so the author has clearly and factu-
ally described both the pleasures and the dangers of
the drug. Neither the author nor the publisher is attempting to encourage the use of cocaine by describing its delights. Nor are they trying to discourage its
use by reporting its drawbacks. Cocaine is already a
part of our reality. Despite the billions of dollars spent

by the government to stop the flow of cocaine into this country, its flow increases. Despite the disproportionately severe legal penalties for the use of cocaine, its popularity grows and has already reached the point where the supply can no longer meet the demand.

As long as people are using cocaine, it is best that they learn to do so safely and pleasurably. It must be emphasized, however, that possession and use of either coca or cocaine is highly illegal in the USA and most other places (an additional danger). It would be unlawful in such places to carry out any of the directions given in this book. The author and publisher are not suggesting that the reader engage in any of the activities described herein. The information contained in this book is given purely for the sake of knowledge. What the reader does with this knowledge is his own responsibility. If any of this information adds to the pleasure and safety of readers who are already using cocaine, this book will have served a morally valid function.

WHAT IS COCAINE? WHAT IS COCA?

Cocaine is an alkaloid contained in the leaves of the South American shrub *Erythroxylon coca* Lam. This plant is native to the eastern curve of the Andes mountains. The shrub normally grows to a height of about 12 feet, but for convenience of harvesting it is kept pruned to 3–6 feet. The leaves also contain other alkaloids related to cocaine. These include ecgonine, cinnamyl cocaine, α- and β-truxilline, hygrine and coca-tannic acid. Several of these substances possess some pharmacological activity, especially when taken in combination with cocaine, but none of them have the powerfully stimulating effects of that drug. Coca has been cultivated rather successfully in Africa and Java, but the greatest amount by far comes from its native Peru and Bolivia. Since pre-Incan times the coca leaf has been used by the Indians of Peru for energy, sustenance and a feeling of well-being. It is generally chewed with a pinch of slaked lime to release the alkaloids. The type of coca leaf cultivated in Peru and preferred there contains a lesser amount of cocaine and a greater amount of the other aromatic alkaloids than the type grown in Bolivia. The Bolivian leaf, called Huanoco leaf, is larger and more oval than the Peruvian leaf (Truxillo leaf), which is proportionately narrower and more lanceolate in shape. The Bolivian shrub is also cultivated at higher altitudes. The leaves cultivated in other places, such as Colombia, Brazil, New Granada, and Java, are as small or smaller than the Peruvian leaf.

Cocaine is derived from the coca leaf by rendering it alkaline and extracting with almost any organic solvent. The free-base alkaloid or alkaloidal mix is then converted into a salt by treatment with an acid. The most commonly used salt is cocaine hydrochloride, although the sulfate, hypochlorate and oxalate are sometimes encountered. The product may be a mixture of hydrochlorides of cocaine and the companion alkaloids, usually referred to as refined cocaine or mixed alkaloidal cocaine. Or it may be further purified to 99–100% pure cocaine hydrochloride. This purified product is known as pharmaceutical quality cocaine. For anesthetic purposes the purified product is definitely superior. The mixed alkaloidal product, however, is usually preferred for hedonistic use. The accompanying alkaloids tend to mellow out the keen but sometimes jagged stimulation of pure cocaine. When a quantitative analysis is run on 100% pure cocaine hydrochloride, it may read as 89% cocaine. This is because the hydrochloride portion occupies 11% of the molecular weight.

Depending upon the method of extraction employed, cocaine may appear as either crystalline flakes or as solid chunks known as rock cocaine. There are varying notions among users of the drug as to the preferability of one form or another. Actually there is no difference in potency between rock and flake cocaine as long as the purity is the same. Still, many dealers will reconstitute their product into one form or another to gratify the illusions of their customers. This is discussed at greater length in the chapter entitled "Purification of Cocaine." Cocaine may also be synthesized. Detailed instructions for doing so are given in *Basic Drug Manufacture*, a Twentieth Century Alchemist publication.

A CONCISE HISTORY OF COCA AND COCAINE

Coca leaves were chewed by pre-Inca tribes of Peru at least 2000, and perhaps 3000, years ago. This fact came to light in 1917 when mummy bundles were discovered in Peruvian tombs. The bundles contained sacks of coca leaves and containers of lime (chewed with coca to release its active principles). Legends of

the pre-Incan Yunga tribe speak of their divine evic-
tion from their capital city, Tiahuanaco, when Khunu,
the god of thunder, lightning and snow, became angry
at them for burning the forests and polluting the world
with smoke and soot. As hungry nomads they found
that coca sustained them in the high Andes until they
were eventually able to return to their city. The Incan
legend tells of how Manco Capac—divine offspring
of the Sun god—taught them to improve their lives,
brought them knowledge and turned them on to the
usefulness of coca. During the earlier part of their
reign the Incas tried to keep the limited supply of coca
to themselves, but before long it was used by all
classes.

In 1531 Pizarro came to Peru and conquered the
Incas. At first the Catholic Spaniards outlawed the
use of coca by the Indians. They regarded coca chewing as an idle practice and believed that its effects were
either imaginary or the result of a pact the Indians
supposedly had with the devil. The conquered people
were put to work mining precious metals for their new
masters. These mines were at high altitudes, and by
1550 the Spaniards realized that they could get more
work out of Indians who chewed the stimulating coca
leaf. The prohibition was promptly revoked.

About this time one of Pizarro's men, Pedro Cieza
de León, published *Crónica del Perú*, which gives
descriptions of the use of coca and perpetuates the
myth of its imaginary or devil-inspired efficacy. In
1556 Nicolas Monardes brought to Europe the first
scientific account of the botany and uses of coca, but
he draws mostly upon Cieza's writings and beliefs. In
1590 Father José de Acosta, a Jesuit, published

Natural History of the Indies and stated that the effects of coca are real, not imaginary. In 1609 Garcilaso de la Vega published *Royal Commentaries of the Incas*, which gives detailed descriptions of the agriculture, curing and use of coca, while attempting to convey to Europeans that coca's effects are real.

During the 17th and 18th centuries Europeans showed very little interest in coca. This was due at least in part to the fact that much of the coca imported to Europe would spoil and lose its potency en route. In 1783 the botanist A. L. Jussieu classed coca properly with the genus *Erythroxylon*, and it was listed in Lamarck's *Encyclopédie Méthodique Botanique* as *Erythroxylon coca*. During the middle 1800s numerous learned visitors to the Andes published praises of coca's great value in sustaining strength while journeying through these rugged altitudes. Mention was even made of its ability to revive waning sexual potency.

In 1859 or 1860 Albert Niemann isolated the alkaloid cocaine from coca, but there is evidence that Gaedecke succeeded in doing the same thing 4 or 5 years earlier. Gaedecke named his alkaloid erythroxyline. Niemann called his cocaine.

In the early 1860s Angelo Mariani of Corsica introduced his elixir *Vin Mariani* to Europe and made a fortune with it. This tonic was a wine containing extracts of coca leaves and several other herbs. It was said to improve vigor and cure or alleviate a host of ailments. Testimonials to its efficacy were given by hundreds of well-known personages including Sarah Bernhardt, Queen Victoria of England, Thomas Edison, Pope Leo XIII, and numerous medical doctors and scientists. After this many coca or cocaine products reached the market, among them pastilles, lozenges, teas, coca leaf cigars and cigarettes, nose sprays and powders, chewing gums, soda pops, and many patent medicines and nostrums. One of the largest of *Vin Mariani's* competitors was *Metcalf's Coca Wine,* which made outlandish claims about its ability to cure various disorders.

During this period, private and professional experimentation with coca or cocaine flourished. The drug was inexpensive and available without prescription in both Europe and America. In 1882 a German medical researcher named Schroff had noted that cocaine caused local numbness when applied to the tip of the tongue. This phenomenon was ignored until 1868 when Thomas Moreno y Maiz, a Peruvian physician, suggested that cocaine might be useful as a local anesthetic. Still, this possibility was not explored until 1884, when Sigmund Freud published his famous paper *Über Coca,* in which he reports in detail the psychopharmacological effects of the drug and suggests several possible medical uses, including use as a treatment for morphine addiction and as a local anesthetic. Freud recommended the latter use to his friend Carl Koller, who in turn demonstrated cocaine's usefulness as an anesthetic for eye surgery. During this same year Dr. William Stewart Halsted of New York found that by injecting cocaine into a nerve trunk, anesthesia of all nerves connected to that trunk occurred. This led to Dr. J. Leonard Corning's idea of using the drug for spinal anesthesia.

During the 1880s enthusiasm over cocaine mounted as reports of its various uses were publicized. There were numerous articles regarding its effectiveness in the treatment of morphine addiction, a concept for which the American Dr. W. H. Bentley deserves the first credit (1878). In 1883 a German army physician, Dr. Theodor Aschenbrandt, gave cocaine to soldiers and found that those who had received it showed greater energy and less fatigue that those who had not. Following through on the public interest in the new wonder drug and on Mariani's success, John Styth Pemberton of Atlanta, Georgia in 1885 created a product called *French Wine Coca–Ideal Nerve and Tonic Stimulant.* A year later he introduced to the public a soft drink syrup made from caffeine and cocaine called *Coca-Cola.*

During the years from 1885 to 1906 there grew a simultaneous boom in the cocaine products industry and a legalistic and moralistic censure of its flagrant use. Many more patent medicines containing substantial amounts of the drug reached the market, but propaganda campaigns were launched to link cocaine use to black, criminal, and poor elements of society. The public attitude towards cocaine became premeditatedly distorted. Under pressure from Southern politicians, Pemberton in 1903 was compelled to take cocaine out of *Coca-Cola.* Today *Coca-Cola* is made of caffeine from kola nuts and decocainized coca leaves.

Between 1887 and 1914 forty-six states passed laws regulating the distribution and use of cocaine. Curiously, during this same period only twenty-nine states passed laws controlling the opiates. Still, products containing cocaine continued to be sold without mention of the drug's presence. In 1906 the Federal Pure

Food and Drug Act was passed. This law required manufacturers to list the contents of their product on the label and almost completely succeeded in preventing the inclusion of cocaine in patent medicines and soft drinks. Then in 1914 the first Federal antidrug law—the Harrison Act—was passed. This law regards cocaine as an extremely dangerous drug and places more controls on it than on the opiates. Nevertheless, cocaine use increased in the USA between 1914 and 1930, while the price of the product on the black market rose steeply.

Meanwhile, political paranoia over cocaine spread to European nations. In 1916 Great Britain passed severe laws against cocaine. Strangely, it was not until four years later that England made similar laws against the opiates.

In the USA the 1922 Amendment to the Narcotic Drugs Import and Export Act erroneously but deliberately classified cocaine as a narcotic. Between this time and the 1960s underground cocaine use continued, but to a rather limited extent and mostly only in New York and other major cities. The amphetamine drugs reached the market in 1932. Being a cheaper and longer-lasting stimulant than cocaine and available either by prescription or on the underground market, their use swept the nation and the world. By the late 1960s, however, members of the counter-culture realized through experience that the amphetamines—especially methedrine—were truly dangerous drugs and began seeking out the much safer cocaine. This brought about a new boom in the illegal cocaine industry. It became the elite stimulant of both the enlightened straight world and the counter-culture. At this time, persecution of marijuana users was in the process of slackening, and authorities began to focus more on enforcing laws against cocaine use. The United States government's Comprehensive Drug Abuse Prevention and Control Act of 1970 intentionally perpetuated the incorrect classification of cocaine as a narcotic.

Between 1972 and 1975 organized crime—especially Cuban groups—began taking over the illicit distribution of cocaine in the USA. Prices soon doubled, while quality dropped steeply. The price of cocaine is now at an all-time high. When Sigmund Freud purchased his first gram of cocaine in 1884, he was displeased to have to pay $1.27 for it. He had expected to pay about 13¢. In 1906 an ounce (28.35 grams) sold for $2.50 in New York. Today the legal price of pharmaceutical cocaine is about $27 per ounce. In 1972 the black market price of an ounce of cocaine was about $900. At the time of this writing (1979) the same amount sells for around $2000.

There are now strong arguments for changing the present cocaine laws and making it available over the counter or at least by prescription in drug stores. Just as ad hoc organizations for the legislation or decriminalization of marijuana, such as LEMAR, NORML and Amorphia, evolved during the past decade, similar groups such as LECOC, bent on doing the same thing for cocaine, are now developing. There is much resistance to be encountered on the road to changing the present restrictions. Many political and law-enforcement groups have vested interests in the illegal traffic of cocaine (and heroin too). Greed is always a powerful adversary to social progress. The

greatest hope is an educated and enlightened public, if
that can ever be arranged.

COCAINE AND THE GOLDEN AGE
OF DECADENCE

We are living in an age of decadence. It cannot be
avoided. It is an inevitable part of history and progress. The everyday demands of survival have slack-
ened. Illusory moral values are in a state of rapid
collapse. Leisure and luxury are becoming more and
more abundant, and this abundance no longer perme-
ates only the upper crust, where it usually resides, but
is seeping downward through the middle and lower
classes.

For many who nurture hopes for the future of our
world, decadence is a frightening word. It conjures
visions of the final days of civilization blackened by
distorted orgies and a sick disregard for life ending in
the deglorification of Greece, the collapse of Rome,
and the angelic or extraterrestrial destruction of
Sodom and Gomorrah. Decadence seems always to be
a prelude to a fall. But then isn't the fall harder, the
higher we climb? It may be that decadence is merely
one of the highest states of civilization and that its
dangers lie only in its vertiginous altitudes.

It is the author's personal philosophy that if there be
any teleological purpose to man's existence on earth
and in his power to progress, it is that he should
achieve a successful form of decadence and learn to
live in harmony with it. The life-game then would be,
at least in part, to sustain a decadent situation for as

long as one might expect any civilization to last and perhaps longer. Such an accomplishment requires a great amount of self-knowledge and the ability to keep positive and negative forces in balance. It is probable that an understanding of Taoist principles would be useful in such an endeavor.

It is not the author's intent to probe in depth the philosophy of decadence at this time, even though he has many profound notions on the subject. Perhaps, if there is enough interest among his readers, he will do so in another book at some future date. The thought is suggested here because cocaine is so much a part of the New Decadence, and, like decadence itself, can either elevate or destroy us, depending entirely upon which we permit it to do.

To live with decadence requires knowledge — roadmaps of the path of jade. That, for the most part, is what this book is about. It is a roadmap of one small segment of the New Kingdom of Decadence in which a person may either find or lose himself. The high roads and low roads of these regions, like the road to Oz, are staggered with threats. Speaking more realistically and a bit less poetically, the path of cocaine as it stands in the streets of today offers dangers not only inherent in the pharmacology of the alkaloid itself, but also in the bizarre assortment of adulterants which are added to it by black market middlemen. This is what happens when a popular substance is made illegal. We have lived this nightmare before and still have not learned. During Prohibition even the cautiously moderate drinker was in danger of unwittingly consuming bootlegger's wood alcohol. Today's drinker is endangered only by his own willingness to

be the fool. The coke snorter, however, finds himself
in much the same position as the average man of the
Prohibition Era. He has no guarantee of what he is
buying. It may contain a fair percentage of cocaine,
but he does not know what substances have been used
to cut it.

This book is a practical guide to the uses and abuses
of cocaine. It contains information on the nature of
cocaine, how to use it and not abuse it, what substances are used to cut it, what the dangers and drawbacks of the various cuts are, how to test for the
presence of certain cuts, and in some cases how to
remove the cuts and purify the cocaine by relatively
simple kitchen procedures. At some date in the near
future it is hoped that these chapters on cuts will
become obsolete or merely of historical interest. This
could only happen if cocaine is legalized and its purity
controlled as is that of other foods, beverages and
drugs that are commercially available. The sooner
this happens, the better, because the Golden Age of
Decadence towards which we are inevitably moving
can succeed without disaster only in an atmosphere of
freedom, knowledge, and respect for the lifestyles of
ourselves and each other.

ENJOYING COCAINE WITHOUT ABUSING IT

EFFECTS OF COCAINE

A few minutes after snorting one or two lines of cocaine, a person will feel the first stimulating effects of the drug. A sensation of energy and euphoria will begin to mount in the body. Within five minutes the full stimulation manifests itself and sensory perceptions are heightened. The mind becomes sharper, the body surges with energy. One is likely to become quite talkative, but, unlike marijuana and hashish, the conversation does not tend towards giddiness and absurdity. Frequently the cannabis drugs make one's being incline towards introspective thinking. Cocaine, however, is generally a more extroverted drug. Under its influence, conversation is likely to be open and realistic. This is not to say that cocaine makes a person feel serious. Cocaine is most definitely a fun drug when used properly. It does not produce hallucinations or distortions of reality. The only distortions or hallucinations associated with cocaine occur from extended and excessive use of it, and these do not stem from the drug itself, but are due to the exhausted state of the mind, body and nervous system. The peak of stimulation usually lasts 20–30 minutes, but residual stimulation may continue for as long as 2 hours. When one comes down from a few snorts there is no "crash" (sudden exhaustion or depression) as with the amphetamine drugs. One may wish to take some more, but there is no craving to do so, and if one does not indulge again at the time, he is quite content with having had a good time.

When a normal dose (20–30 mg) of cocaine is taken there is a vasoconstrictive action affecting the blood vessels and the heart. Curiously, minute doses (5–10 mg) will slow the heart and pulse rate, whereas normal doses (20–30 mg) will increase it. Extremely large doses, of course, are dangerous, and, if large enough, may result in cardiac arrest. When normal doses are taken, blood pressure rises at first, but returns to normal after a while. Body temperature may also rise slightly and muscular energy is somewhat increased. After a moderate dose the user may notice feelings of increased energy, mental clarity, euphoria, improved muscular strength, sexual stimulation, and a reduction of both appetite and fatigue. Such properties are of unquestionable value if the drug is used properly. If used to improper excess—that is, if too much is taken at one time or if moderate doses are taken continuously over too long a period without a break—many of these desirable effects can become distorted or reversed.

Cocaine has several minor side effects worth noting. It often acts as a mild laxative. A few snorts have been known to relieve constipation within an hour or two. It also has diuretic properties. While using cocaine a person often has to urinate more frequently and more copiously than usual. Another characteristic of cocaine is that it tends to dry out the mucous membranes. This can be helpful if the nasal passages are congested. But if the membranes remain dry for too long a time, irritations may ensue.

AVOIDING THE ABUSIVE POTENTIAL OF COCAINE

Cocaine is the drug of the true hedonist. It is compatible with almost any pleasure, whether it be of the mind or the body. It is a sacrament for those who are masters and mistresses of their own pleasures. Unlike alcohol, heroin, and tobacco, it is not for those who are slaves to their needs and desires. It does not have the addictive potential of the opiates and barbiturates. If a person has been enjoying cocaine on a regular basis and suddenly his supply is cut off, he may be disappointed, but he won't be climbing the walls. Still, cocaine, like almost any other pleasure, has its potential for misuse and abuse. It is possible to overdo it or to develop a psychological dependence upon it. But one can do the same with many other enjoyable things. Food or exercise can be overdone, and one can become psychologically dependent upon sex, TV, and religion.

If taken in moderation or if excessive use is merely occasional, cocaine can be a most enjoyable addition to one's life. But if it is used to improper excess, it can be injurious to both mental and physical health. The important thing is to know when you have had enough, and to stop and take a break before going beyond this point. It is also valuable to take measures during such a break to bring the body back to normal once more. In this chapter we will not only examine the many ways in which cocaine may be enjoyed, but also the dangers inherent in the drug and how to circumvent them.

There is some difference of opinion among users as to how much use goes beyond the bounds of moderation. Some people use one or two doses each day of their life and regard this as moderate. Others prefer to get deeper into the drug but less frequently. One person may use more than one gram in the course of a single evening and not touch it again for several weeks. Some feel that 250–500 mg per day for several days followed by a break of at least as many days is a safe and prudent way to enjoy the drug.

Although the precise measurements of moderation and excess may vary among individuals, there is universal agreement as to the warning signals of overuse. Among the first signs are edginess, impatience, mild insomnia, excessive and often cold sweating, general loss of appetite, pallor and occasional impotence. One may also have feelings of lassitude in the morning, much like those from an alcohol hangover. When these symptoms first appear it is best to curtail the use of cocaine and take steps for recuperation and revitalization as described later in this chapter. If these initial warning signals are not heeded, continued use will lead to even worse symptoms. Edginess will progress to anxiety, aggressive behavior, and possible personality changes and paranoia. Tactile hallucinations (crawly feelings on the skin) may even occur. Insomnia and impotence will become more extreme. Early morning hangover will extend to all-day depression and heaviness of the limbs.

It is probable that most people would not continue far beyond this point. Anyone who does is taking gambles with his health and will take a much longer time to fully recuperate than one who has stopped at the first warning signals. The master hedonist does not let his pleasure encroach upon his well-being. Cocaine, of course, is not addicting. Still, it is very tempting to continue its use after lassitude has developed, and it is time to stop. For a day or two a person may miss the buoyant energies to which he has become accustomed. If there is depression, he knows that he can relieve it with just a little snort. But this relief is short-lasting, and when depression returns it will be even deeper, and another snort will be called for, and so on.

Not many people continue beyond this point unless there is a predisposition towards self-destruction in their nature. But few people have enough sense to stop at the first signals. The sooner one does take a break the sooner he will be able to resume this and other decadent pleasures. Even the most hard-core coke user respects the fact that he must pace his usage of the drug if he is to enjoy its benefits and avoid its discomforts.

TAKING A BREAK

Cocaine is a most powerful central nervous system stimulant. The CNS is a very delicate structure. Relentless stimulation leads to disruption of its function and possible damage. If there are indications that disruption has begun to occur, not only must the cause itself (in this case cocaine) be eliminated, but so should any other factors which have a similar effect, even to a lesser degree. This includes the heavy use of coffee, tobacco and alcohol, as well as any of the more powerful stimulants, such as amphetamines and psychedelics. Moderate use of cannabis is generally safe as a relaxant.

Adequate sleep and relaxation plus regular and wholesome meals are essential to recovery. Yoga or moderate exercise is most helpful. If insomnia symptoms persist, one should try to avoid barbiturates and other powerful sedatives as much as possible. One is trying to rebuild the nervous system, and frequent use of most of these drugs defeats the purpose. Hot baths or saunas are often effective in producing the desired state of relaxation. They also assist in ridding the body of the toxic residues of exhaustion. One should not stay in the bath or sauna longer than 15 minutes at a time. Bear in mind that cocaine places some stress upon the heart. Hot baths or saunas, if prolonged, can add to that strain.

Vitamins C and B complex are depleted in the body during heavy cocaine usage. They should be taken not only throughout the revitalization period but also during an extended period of cocaine snorting. Since cocaine reduces appetite, one may not feel like eating as much food as the body really needs, but vitamin intake should be maintained. Vitamin C assists in the removal of toxic wastes from the body. B complex vitamins help to rebuild the nervous system and restore energies. Vitamin E is also of value because it improves heart response at a time when that organ is under some stress. Many veteran snorters take ginseng before, during and after a cocaine run (an extended binge). It seems to lessen the unpleasant side effects and hasten revitalization. In short: after a coke run go on a health kick.

When you start to feel like your normal healthy self again you may want to indulge in the pleasures of cocaine once more. Don't. Not right away. Give your poor body a break. The more time that elapses between heavy usage, the better. Remember: your body is an instrument of pleasure. To fulfill its purpose and to enjoy its possibilities completely it—like any instrument—must be kept in tune and proper condition.

THE NOSE KNOWS

Aside from the subtle injury that severe abuse of cocaine can do to the nervous system and the body in general, there is also the more obvious corrosive damage that it can do to the mucous membranes of the nose and throat. Long-term continuous and excessive use of cocaine has been known eventually to damage the olfactory ganglia responsible for the sense of smell and has occasionally resulted in perforation of the septum—the portion that separates the nasal passages. Some people may be less susceptible to the drug's corrosive action than others, but none are completely immune.

Cocaine granules can also lodge in the hair follicles of the nostrils, causing sores, boils and possible nose bleeding. Some of the substances used to cut coke are even worse offenders in this respect than the drug itself. The more finely the cocaine is pulverized before snorting, the less likely are the granules to lodge in these follicles or to linger upon the mucous membranes. Dilution of cocaine in water, as described under Liquid Lady in the next chapter, is the safest method of taking cocaine into the nostrils. The corrosiveness of cocaine is greatly reduced by this method and the possibility of getting granules in the follicles is virtually nonexistent.

Many serious coke snorters make a practice of snorting a few drops of water into the nostrils about 15 minutes after having a hit of coke. This allows enough time for most of the drug to be absorbed into the tissues before washing the residues away. Nose drops or nasal sprays are also useful towards this end. Nasal douches are available at some head shops. These are tiny glass vessels which hold just enough water for one cleansing snort.

Some people, not wishing to give up the pleasures of cocaine for even a little while when the nose and throat become irritated, will switch to a different route of intake, such as smearing it between the gums or under the tongue, ingesting it with alcohol, or even injecting it. The best advice, however, is if the nose says that it has had enough, the rest of the body has also had its fill.

Another way to douche the nostrils is to immerse a plastic straw about 2 inches in water, place a finger over the top of the straw, remove the straw from the water, tilt back the head, insert the lower part of the straw into the nostril, and remove the finger while snorting the water. Some people prefer to put ½ tsp. of water in a teaspoon, tilt back the head, place the front of the spoon against the nostril, and snort the water. Gargling with water at about the same time as douching the nostrils is advised to protect the throat from soreness. After douching the nostrils, vitamin E oil can be applied to the nasal passages with a Q-tip. This helps to speed the healing of sore membranes.

OVERDOSE AND ALLERGIC SENSITIVITY

Although cocaine is a safe and enjoyable drug when used wisely, it has its potential dangers. We have already discussed the possibilities of excessive use over an extended period of time. Two other dangers are overdose and allergic sensitivity. Very few people are allergic to cocaine (less than are allergic to penicillin), but anyone can overdose if he is foolish enough to take too much at one time. The amount of cocaine that will result in overdose symptoms varies with the individual. The average lethal dose is estimated at 1.2 grams taken within half an hour's time. Although some people have taken this much or even more without fatal results, many more have succumbed to smaller quantities.

The first symptoms of overdose may include increased blood pressure and heart-pulse rate, rapid but shallow breathing, blue skin color, convulsions and fainting. The second set of symptoms—appearing several minutes later—may include muscular paralysis, loss of reflex, loss of consciousness, respiratory failure marked by ashen-gray skin color, circulatory collapse with little or no detectable pulse, cardiovascular collapse, and death. If these symptoms occur, they will do so soon after taking the drug and will in a short time either run their course or result in death. Professional medical attention is indicated, but it is unlikely to be received in time. Treatment must begin as soon as the first signs of overdose appear. Since there are two stages of reaction to overdose, each must be treated separately at the proper times. The first stage is marked by overstimulation; the second by understimulation. While the initial symptoms are happening the victim should be kept cool and exposed to fresh air. He should sit on a floor or bed with knees raised and head lowered between them (Trendelenburg position). If convulsions occur and a person qualified to give injections is present, small amounts of a short-acting barbiturate such as sodium pentothal (25–50 mg) may be injected intravenously. If convulsions persist, the treatment may be cautiously repeated. One must be careful, however, that the depressant effects of the barbiturate do not carry over into the next stage. After the initial overstimulation symptoms have passed, reverse shock may be expected. Trendelenburg position should be maintained. Arms and legs should be wrapped in blankets to increase the return of blood to central areas. Back massage is helpful. Injection of a cardiotonic stimulant such as phenylephrine (10–20 mg *i.v.*) may be indicated. During the entire ordeal the victim's vital signs should be carefully watched. Unless the victim already has a cardiac problem, respiratory failure usually occurs before heart failure. If breathing stops, artificial respiration must be given immediately until breathing is resumed. One should rest for at least three hours after recovery and not use cocaine again for several weeks (see comments below regarding induced sensitivity).

Although it is rare, some individuals may be allergic to cocaine. Upon taking even a small amount of the drug they may suffer severe reactions. It has already been mentioned that the average lethal dose is about 1.2 grams. 20–50 mg is usually a safe but effective dose. If one is allergic to cocaine, this small amount may be enough to cause anaphylactic shock, overdose symptoms, and possible death. Anaphylactic sensitivity is usually an inherent condition. It may also occur if a person has had a serious overdose experience and recovered. In this instance induced anaphylactic sensitivity may develop. This is similar to the well-known phenomenon in which the person who recovers from the stings of a swarm of bees is stung at some later date by a single bee and dies. Although anaphylactic response is not common, caution is always a worthy ally. If one is trying cocaine for the first time or if one has had a severe previous overdose experience, it is best that he test himself with a small amount of cocaine (¼ line), wait half an hour, increase the dose to half a line, wait another half hour, increase to a whole line, wait half an hour and increase to the normal two-line dose. If no undesirable symptoms are experienced, one may be safely assured that he does not suffer from anaphylactic sensitivity to cocaine.

COCAINE, ALCOHOL AND DOWNERS

Many people smoke, drink or take tranquilizers, sedatives or narcotics with cocaine to counterbalance the tension and agitation from large doses of the drug. The danger in doing this lies in the masking of the cocaine effects by a depressant. For instance, if much alcohol is consumed its depressant effects may override the cocaine stimulation, and a person would be inclined to snort more coke to the point of overdosing. The same may occur when using opiates, barbiturates or other powerful sedation drugs at the same time as using cocaine. Nevertheless, the judicious combination of cocaine with these drugs can be most pleasant. A popular device to achieve this is known as the speedball. It consists of a dose of cocaine with a dose of heroin or morphine. The result of snorting this combination is an initial coke rush leveling off after about 15 minutes as the slower-acting opiates take effect. After this the heroin sedation deepens and the user experiences "the roller coaster ride"; that is, a periodic up and down alternation between the effects of the two drugs. During the '60s amphetamines were often used in place of cocaine. Today cocaine and heroin are frequently combined. However, the combination of cocaine or an amphetamine with a barbiturate is also common.

THE PLEASURES OF COCAINE

Cocaine is a drug that combines well with most other pleasures except perhaps eating and sleeping. While one is under the effects, it usually acts as a deterrent to sleep and appetite, but fortunately these effects are short-lasting—about two hours.

COCAINE AND SEX

There has been much talk of cocaine as an erotic drug or aphrodisiac. We present here some excerpts from the entry on Cocaine in another of the author's books, *The Encyclopedia of Sex Drugs and Aphrodisiacs.*

Of all the illegal drugs, cocaine is the one most often regarded as a sex drug. A snort or two of cocaine can give a person tremendous sexual energy. A man who has taken cocaine may find himself maintaining erection even after one or more orgasms. The drug also tends to give a man great control over orgasm. This is valuable in chronic cases of premature ejaculation and may be of some use to persons who are trying to develop control in Tantric sex techniques. Even after many orgasms a man who has taken cocaine may still be semi-hard and able to enjoy karezza, the practice of long, sustained intercourse in which the two partners barely move their bodies but rely upon the more subtle movements of the pulsations and quiverings of the sexual organs. The ability of cocaine to permit lengthy intercourse is so positive that it is advisable to make use of a lubricant during such episodes. The female glands which provide lubrication usually dry out before the experience is completed.

Sometimes, depending upon the individual and his mood, cocaine may have an opposite effect upon sexual desire and performance. Occasionally the drug will so greatly stimulate the intellectual centers of the mind that the brain will fairly reel with hyperactive thought. This can detract from sensual desire to the extent that all the person may want to do is think or talk out his thoughts. Cocaine can be a very "talkative" drug. This can be annoying to a lover if the subject matter is not of an intimate nature. Most often, however, the talkativeness manifests itself as openness and willing communication of personal feelings. People who are into kinky sex (offbeat, unusual or even bizarre sexual experimentation which the taboo-scarred members of our society call perverted) find cocaine the ideal drug to put them in the mood for such pleasures.

Many coke-and-sex fans claim that smoking cocaine is better for sex than snorting it. It is said to be more effective and reliable in prolonging endurance this way. However, it is not as stoning and its effects do not last as long (about 1–2 hours of smoking compared to 2–4 hours of snorting).

Aside from its internal use for stimulating the brain, nervous system and musculature, cocaine is also applied topically as a surface anesthetic to desensitize certain areas of the body. It is sometimes mixed with a little water or ointment and applied to the head and shaft of the penis to decrease sensation and prevent premature ejaculation. Cocaine ointment is also used to make anal intercourse easier, and in cases of painful vaginal intercourse. Sometimes after one or more orgasms a woman's clitoris will become so sensitive that further stimulation is irritating. A little cocaine on the clitoris will anesthetize this surface irritation and enable the woman to enjoy many more orgasms. Because there is no sensation in the superficial nerves when this is done, the ensuing orgasms are experienced at more profound levels than usual and are more intense and soul-shattering. Because of the current high price of cocaine it is more economical to use one of the several other less expensive related benzoic esters, such as benzocaine or butacaine sulfate. There are several products in the form of ointments and aerosol sprays that are designed for these purposes. They usually sell for about $5 per ½ ounce in adult stores and through mail order. A product called *Solarcaine,* which is used for relieving the pain of sunburn and other surface injuries, is available from any pharmacy or supermarket health aid shelf for about $2.50 per 5-ounce can. It can be used for any of the above-mentioned purposes.

In Peru it is coca leaves rather than cocaine that the Indians use daily. The two ounces of leaves that the average Indian chews each day with a piece of slaked lime to release the alkaloids contain about ½ gram of cocaine. Most medical experts who have knowledge of this drug maintain that the leaves are much better than the extracted alkaloid. Homeopathic doctors have often prescribed small doses of coca leaves in cases of physical exhaustion due to sexual excesses.

As it was pointed out in the above excerpts, sometimes cocaine affects certain individuals in such a manner that, instead of exciting sexual desire, it stimulates the cerebral centers. When this happens a person may not at all wish to indulge in erotic activities, but will prefer to exercise the mind with conversation, contemplation or even study. Sometimes, too, a person may feel sexually aroused from the stimulation of cocaine, but may not have a desirable sex partner available at the moment. In that case, unless the person wishes to indulge in the solitary joys of masturbation (which can be most rewarding and enlightening under the spell of cocaine), it may be preferred to rechannel these libidinous energies into some intellectual pursuit such as acting, puzzle-solving, intelligent or even intellectual discussion, music-making, or study. Because alertness is increased under cocaine, retention of learned materials is often improved.

COCAINE AND THE
LEARNING PROCESSES

Used properly, cocaine can be an excellent adjunct to learning. The important thing in using cocaine as a study aid is not to overdo it. The mind is only made of flesh. The stimulation that the drug offers the mind may tempt the user to exploit its effects beyond sensible limits. This could have a reverse effect, resulting in confusion rather than clarity.

If cocaine is to be employed to enhance learning, it is recommended that the mind and body (including the eyes) be well rested at the time. The duration of the study period should be scheduled beforehand and not exceeded. With so much stimulation going on, and the source of it lying before one on the snorting tray, it is tempting to push onward into the night. There is a point, however, when the mind and body will be exhausted, but the stimulation will not allow one to realize that this is so. If study is continued in this state, it is possible for the mind to distort the data which it is receiving and retain it wrongly in the memory.

The best results are gained by engaging in an intense and undistracted study period for the approximately two hours that one dose of the drug affects. Then take a thorough rest for at least two more hours before engaging in further study with cocaine. If you are studying on a regular basis, do not use cocaine for more than one such study period daily.

If you are using cocaine to cram for an exam (generally not a good idea), it may be necessary to border on excessive use of the drug. If you go even a little too far with it, this could defeat your purpose. If you have been up several nights coking and cramming, you may start to get a bit delirious with your studies. And, what is worse, when you go to the classroom on the date of the exam, you may find yourself in such an exhausted and befuddled state that it might almost have been

better not to have studied at all. The best pattern for
scholastic use is to take one or two snorts no more
than once a day as needed for especially difficult
studies, review your studies under it two days before
the exam, review the work without cocaine on the eve
of the exam, get plenty of rest that night, and, if necessary, have a moderate dose (a line or two) right before
taking the exam. Some students take pemoline, the
memory drug, with cocaine before an exam. For more
information on this see *Pemoline* in the section on
adulterants.

COCAINE AND PHYSICAL ACTIVITY

Cocaine can also be used to assist one in physical
work and athletics. When this is done rightly, one may
be quite surprised at the improvements in muscular
energy, coordination, breath conservation and endurance. In *History of Coca—The Divine Plant of the
Incas*, W. Golden Mortimer, M.D. reports that around
the turn of the century, on a day that the temperature
was 100 degrees in the sun, members of the Toronto
La Crosse Club, a group of amateurs accustomed to
sedentary work, chewed a small amount of coca leaf
before and during a game against a team of sturdy men
used to outdoor labor and exercise. Before the game
had ended, the rugged team was exhausted, whereas
the sedentary men showed no signs of fatigue. Travel-
ers in the Andes frequently comment on how coca
eases the journey through the mountains. Dr. Benja-
min F. Gibb, U.S.N., in this report on coca to the U.S.

government, attributes this to coca's direct stimulation of the cardiac muscle. It also augments respiratory power and helps the body to make more efficient use of oxygen.

When cocaine is taken and one engages in labor, sports or other physical activities, the euphoric effects disappear quite rapidly and the period of stimulation is shortened. This is because the drug is more swiftly metabolized under these conditions. However, if one is getting into a consistent and rhythmic pattern with any of these activities, as often happens with dancing, swimming, jogging, hiking, and repetitive (but not boring) labor, one may notice a kind of ecstatic feeling of flowing with the movement which can enhance the euphoric properties of the cocaine.

Because of its rapid metabolism in situations of physical exertion, a person can usually take somewhat more of the drug than usual without suffering the side effects and aftereffects of immoderate use. But one should be cautious not to let the stimulation lead to overexertion of the body. The object of using cocaine for physical activity is to give the heart, lungs and muscles a slight edge of improvement, not to attempt to turn the ordinary person into a temporary superbeing who astonishes the world, but burns himself out in a single contest.

METHODS OF USE

Since cocaine is fairly rapidly absorbed through the nasal membranes, one of the most popular ways of using it is to snort it. There are several ways to accomplish this, but the two most frequent methods are from a coke spoon and through a straw or similar cylindrical device. For the safest, most economical and most effective results, certain points in the preparation and use of the cocaine should be attended to.

PREPARING COCAINE FOR SNORTING

Cocaine, as it usually arrives from the dealer, is in the form of crystalline rocks or flakes. These must be pulverized before they are snorted. The reason for this is that the large particles do not absorb as rapidly as the fine powder. Slow absorption causes a delayed and weakened high lacking the much desired coke rush. Also, the longer these crystals linger in the nostrils the more apt they are to do corrosive damage to the delicate nasal membranes.

One of the most common methods of preparing cocaine is to pour it on a mirror and chop it repeatedly with a single-edge razor blade. This is the most time-consuming and least efficient method. Each chopping merely reduces the crystals to ½ or ¼ their original size and often gets them all over the place. We do not recommend it and only mention it because it is so frequently done.

One of the best ways to pulverize the crystals is to pour ⅛–¼ gram of cocaine on a small mirror or other hard, flat, non-porous surface. Crush the crystals to a powder with the rounded bottom of a teaspoon or the top of a Zippo lighter. After being crushed, the mass of powdered cocaine will be stuck together. It then is lightly chopped and fluffed with a single-edge razor blade. Repeat the process of crushing, chopping and

fluffing several more times until the particles are as fine as possible.

Cocaine may also be pulverized in a small ceramic mortar. Crush the crystals with the pestle, then fluff and scrape down the sides with a small plastic straw. Repeat this several times until a fine powder is obtained. Then it is ready to transfer to a mirror or coke spoon for snorting. Some people like to snort it right out of the mortar using a straw.

The most practical commercially available device for pulverizing cocaine is an item sold in most head paraphernalia stores, known as the Snowduster. This reasonably priced device quickly and easily reduces the coke to a fine powder by passing it through a nylon mesh. If it cannot be found locally, it can be ordered from the manufacturer. This company has many other useful items for the cocaine connoisseur. Their catalogue can be obtained by sending $1.00 to Snowduster, 15155 Stagg Street, Van Nuys, CA 91405.

PREPARING THE NOSTRILS

The nostrils should be cleared before snorting. Some connoisseurs go to the extent of douching their nostrils with water or baking soda solution to clear the nasal passages before snorting cocaine. Generally all that is needed is a good nose blow in a handkerchief, or at most a few drops of any good nasal decongestant such as Neo-synephrine.

Don't try to snort though a clogged nostril. Coke is too expensive to waste. If you want to open a nostril, but nose sprays and handkerchiefs have failed, press the ball of your finger against the nose on the opposite side and close off that nostril. Hold this for a minute or so while attempting to breathe through the clogged passage. When it has cleared, blow your nose and then get down to the business of snorting.

Another method of opening a nostril is derived from Tantric practices. The balled fist or a tennis ball is held snugly in the armpit opposite the clogged nostril (left armpit for right nostril). Clutch the fist or ball hard and breathe normally. Within a few minutes the obstruction should clear. This works because of principles similar to those which make acupuncture work.

SETTING UP LINES

When cocaine is properly powdered and the nostrils cleared, one is ready to snort. With the aid of a single-

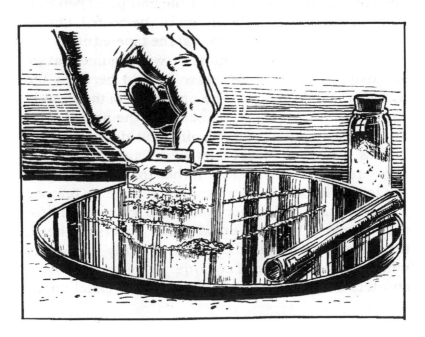

edge razor blade the cocaine is arranged in lines upon a mirror or similar surface. A line is a long pile of cocaine about the size and shape of a paper match; that is, about ⅛ inch wide by 1 inch long. Two lines are gathered for each person; one per nostril.

SNORTING THE COCAINE

A line of cocaine can be snorted through a section of plastic soda straw or any similar cylindrical device, such as a rolled-up dollar bill, a piece of glass or metal tubing, the hull of a ball point pen, or whatever is available. The requirements of a snorting device are that it be ³/₁₆ to ¼ inch in diameter, 2½ to 3 inches long, and smooth enough on the inside that the cocaine does not get trapped within. If the ball point pen hull is used, the wide end should go in the nostril. Otherwise the coke may get trapped at the tapered end.

For purposes of description we will assume that we are using a straw. The straw is held between the thumb and index finger. The upper end of the straw is carefully inserted about ½ inch into the nostril or as far as possible without scraping the delicate membranes. This is to insure that the cocaine reaches the membranous upper nostrils rather than be wasted in the less absorbent lower passages. A finger is pressed gently against the other nostril to close it off for the moment. One then exhales and lowers the head, bringing the bottom of the straw lightly in contact with one end of a line of cocaine. At this point novice snorters frequently make the mistake of exhaling al-

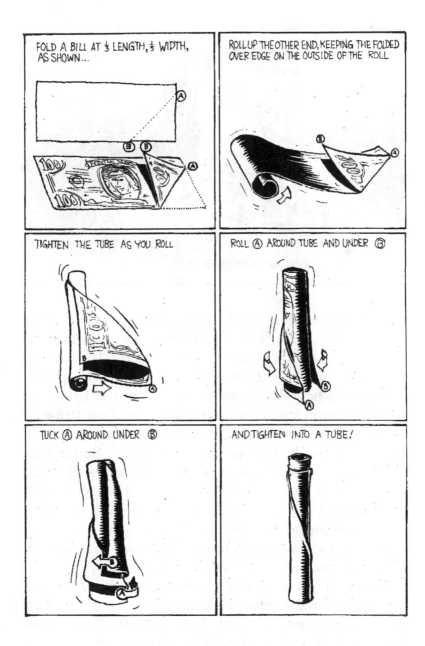

most imperceptibly and blowing the lines all over the place. This is one reason why one should exhale before getting his face close to the cocaine. If you have long hair or a beard, see that it doesn't get into the cocaine. When the straw is touching the line, one inhales abruptly while moving the base of the straw up the line. When inhaling, try to aim the coke far back into the nostrils, but not into the lungs. Some consumers will take the line in a rapid series of short snorts; others in one long smooth snort. Experiment to find what method suits you the best. Any cocaine dust adhering to the mirror after the line is gone is picked up by moving the base of the straw in a circular or zig-zag motion over it while snorting deeply.

When all of a line is taken in, remove the straw and breathe normally through the mouth for a moment. You will notice a mild and not unpleasant smarting in the upper nasal passages that almost seems to penetrate to the brain. Consumers expect good cocaine to "wing" the nostrils in this way. The winging sensation will soon be followed by a freezing or numbing of the nostril and the initial rush of cocaine stimulation. Do not blow your nose and try not to sneeze. If you do so, cocaine will be expelled and wasted. If the nose starts to run, tilt the head back and breathe in sharply. If more cocaine is desired—which is usually the case—the straw is inserted in the other nostril and the process repeated. During the next few minutes the coke high will come on fully. If it does not come on sufficiently, wait about 15 minutes to give what you have taken a chance to assimilate. Then snort another line or two if needed.

Many people make the mistake of greedily snorting one line on top of another as if in a desperate attempt to get their high. It is better to take a little every fifteen minutes or so until the desired high is reached. This caution is especially important if one is a novice or if the cocaine sample is new and untried.

To snort the product with a coke spoon, dip the spoon into a pile of well-pulverized cocaine and take up a well-rounded cokespoonful of it. Don't pick up so much that the powder is on the verge of spilling from the spoon. If the spoon is too full, shake it gently or tap it lightly over the coke container. Remember, you have to get both the spoon and its contents into your nostril without it colliding with your nose.

People have nostrils of different shapes and sizes. If you are new at snorting, try putting the coke spoon in your nose in front of a mirror. If you can flare your nostrils, you have it made. If the entrances to your nostrils are narrow, find the best way to open them.

Place a finger on the nose above the nostril and draw the skin upward; or at the point where the nose and cheek meet, and draw the skin outward; or outward and upward; or below the nostril and draw the skin downward (especially helpful if your mustache is in the way); or whatever opens your nasal entrance the right way for inserting the spoon. Once you have found out what works best for you, a mirror will no longer be needed. Insert the spoon about ¼–½ inch while tilting the head slightly backwards and closing off the opposite nostril with a finger. Snort. Then pause a minute before doing the other nostril.

Many objects have been substituted for coke spoons: a piece of matchbook cover, flat or folded V-wise down the middle; a nail file; the small blade of a pocketknife (be careful); or anything that can hold some cocaine and fit into the nostril. Coke spoons are available at any head shop for about $1.50 each. They often come on a chain and can be worn about the neck like an amulet. Expensive coke spoons are also available in gold or silver and set with precious gems.

A unique but efficient way of snorting cocaine is derived from a method used by South American Indians for taking the hallucinogenic cohoba bark. It requires the assistance of another person. A full-length soda straw is loaded at one end with the equivalent of a line of cocaine. The index finger is held at the opening so that nothing is spilled. The person to receive the hit tilts his head back so that his nasal passages are horizontal. The empty end of the straw is inserted about ½ inch into one of his nostrils. Keeping the straw horizontal, the finger is removed and the mouth of the assisting person is applied to that end

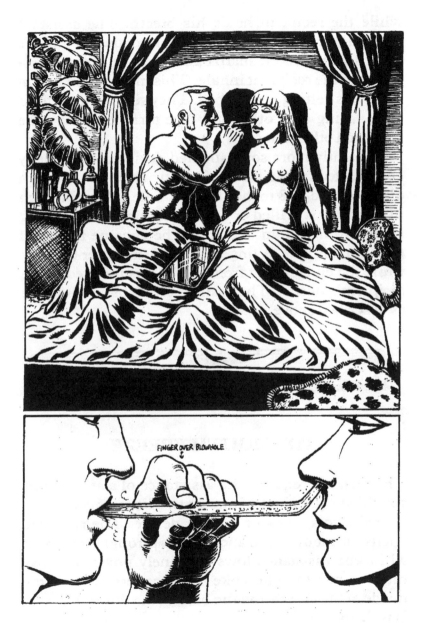

while the recipient holds his breath. The assistant then blows the pile of cocaine into the recipient's nostril with a short, sharp exhalation. It is not necessary that the recipient inhale. This method can be fun for lovers getting high in bed. They simply lie on their sides facing each other and take turns blowing coke into each other's nostrils.

A slightly more sophisticated device can be easily constructed from a piece of plastic tubing ¼–⅜ inch diameter and 6–8 inches long. A hole at least $^3/_{16}$ inch in diameter is drilled or cut on one side of the tubing about an inch from one end. The cocaine is loaded through this hole. A finger is held firmly over the hole while the end farthest from the hole is inserted in the recipient's nostril. The assistant then blows the coke as described above.

THE MOUTH FREEZE

This method requires the assistance of a second person. The equivalent of one or two lines of cocaine is loaded into a straw or similar device. The recipient opens his mouth wide and inhales through the mouth while the assistant blows the finely powdered coke into his mouth. The coke dust scatters all over the inside of the mouth and the back of the throat, where it is well absorbed.

OTHER IMPLEMENTS

New instruments are constantly being designed for snorting cocaine. Y-shaped glass snorters are available at most head shops. With one of these a person can snort cocaine into both nostrils at once. Another item known as the LiL-TOOT is now sold at many head shops. It has a cylindrical space in which cocaine is stored. When the user pushes the spring-operated plunger at the base, a hit of cocaine is brought forward to the chamber and can then be snorted from the instrument. With the LiL-TOOT one may snort cocaine in public or out of doors in the wind without risking loss or discovery.

The Indians of the Amazon sometimes use the hollow, V-shaped breast-bone of birds to self-administer hallucinogenic snuffs. The snuff is dropped into the device. The user inserts one end into his nostril and the other between his lips. He then blows abruptly through his mouth and the snuff is shot into his nose. A similar instrument for the modern cocaine snuffer could be built of glass, plastic, copper, gold or silver.

LIQUID LADY

There are many situations in which snorting with a spoon or straw would not be advisable: in public places where it would be too obvious, out of doors where a sudden breeze could blow your precious product all over the place, dark movie theaters where it can be accidentally spilled. The best way to cope with

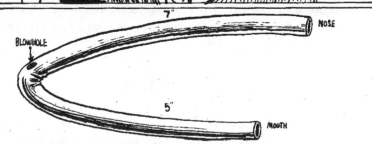

USING AN ALUMINUM TUBE ¼ - ½ INCH IN DIAMETER, FILL WITH DRY SAND, SEAL ENDS TIGHTLY, AND GENTLY BEND OVER A GAS FLAME. DRILL HOLE IN POSITION SHOWN. TO USE, DROP COKE IN BLOWHOLE, THEN USE AS SHOWN IN ILLUSTRATION, KEEPING FINGER OVER BLOWHOLE.

such problems is to dissolve the cocaine in water and snort it as a liquid from a nasal spray bottle.

To do this correctly some attention to measurements must be given. A gram of cocaine makes 30–40 lines. After emptying and rinsing a nasal spray bottle (Neo-synephrine or any similar product is perfect), fill it with plain water and see how many squirts it gives. If it holds 30–40 squirts, it will take a gram of cocaine and give the equivalent of one line per squirt. If the squirt count is more or less than this number, you can adjust the cocaine or water content accordingly.

To prepare the cocaine solution, half fill the bottle with water or a 4-to-1 water/vodka solution. It is best if the water is warm, as it will dissolve the cocaine more easily. Distilled water is preferred to tap water because the hard mineral content of the latter can be troublesome to the sinuses. Add the cocaine and shake well until all of the crystals are thoroughly dissolved. Fill the remainder of the bottle with water and you're ready to go.

Shake the bottle well each time before using. Insert the nozzle in the nostril and squeeze the bottle while snorting lightly. Get the liquid into the upper nasal passages, but not into the throat. Don't take too much at once or repeat too soon or you will have the liquid running down your throat.

Another advantage of this method of use is that the diluted cocaine is less likely to do corrosive damage to the nasal membranes than the powder.

A METHOD FOR MUTANTS

One out of perhaps 50,000 people have extremely flexible tongues that they can curl backward and upward behind the palate and place in the throat behind the nasal passages. If you, like the author, are one of these freaks of nature, you can take advantage of your deformity when using cocaine. Simply place a dab of coke on the tip of the tongue, curl the tongue backward into the throat, being careful not to let the powder brush against the palate, shove the tongue tip into the nasal chamber, and smear the drug evenly in this region. If you can do it, this method is excellent when the nostrils are impossibly clogged. Many yogis are able to do this, but, alas, so few yogis appreciate cocaine.

INTRABUCCAL AND SUBLINGUAL USE

The tissues between the cheeks and the gums and the area beneath the tongue absorb many drugs quite efficiently, though not as well as do the nasal membranes. A dab of cocaine can be picked up on a dampened index finger tip and smeared evenly in either or both of these places. Allow at least 15 minutes for the coke to absorb before eating, drinking or chewing gum.

COCAINE CORDIAL

It was previously believed that one of the least effective routes for cocaine absorption is through the gut, but recent studies show that it is very well assimilated this way. One of the best methods for ingestion is to combine it with an alcoholic beverage, preferably a cordial such as Chartreuse, Benedictine or Galliano. The alcohol and sugar in the cordial are absorbed swiftly in the stomach and serve as a vehicle to assist the assimilation of the cocaine before the digestive fluids can destroy it. To prepare a coke cordial, thoroughly dissolve a gram of cocaine in a pint of the selected liqueur. One tiny cordial glass, or even half a glass, is sufficient for a fine high that comes on within five minutes. We advise that you not overindulge in this drink. The cocaine is made extremely potent by the presence of the alcohol. Half a bottle of this can be dangerous and even lethal. Also, the depressant effects of alcohol combat the stimulating properties of cocaine. If a lot of alcohol is consumed, one may not feel the cocaine and unwittingly take an excessive quantity of the drug. The Cocaine Cordial is a delightful diversion on occasion. But when cocaine is taken internally over a period of time—even several days— it may have an irritating effect upon some stomachs. If one is using cocaine daily, it is better to alternate between oral consumption and snorting.

THE COKE SMOKE

You can get high by smoking cocaine. Quantity for quantity it is not quite as stoning to smoke it as it is to snort it, and the high lasts only half as long. However, people who enjoy combining coke and sex often feel that cocaine taken this way is far more of an aphrodisiac than when it is snorted. It is also said to be more effective and reliable for prolonged sexual endurance when smoked.

There are four basic ways to smoke cocaine:

1) One or two lines of cocaine are sprinkled evenly on the grass or herb in a joint right before it is rolled. Usually no cocaine is sprinkled on the last half inch of grass at the end which is to be held in the mouth. This is done so that none is wasted.

2) On a cigarette: A cigarette (or a joint rolled as perfectly as one) is held in the mouth while the unlit end is placed against a small pile of cocaine. Upon inhaling, some of the cocaine is drawn into the cigarette tip. It is then lighted. The smoke is inhaled and retained in the lungs for a minute.

3) In a pipe: Some cocaine is sprinkled on top of the tobacco or other herb in a pipe. The smoke is inhaled and held.

4) From foil: A piece of aluminum foil is cantilevered from the neck of a bottle. A hollow is made in a portion of the foil with a finger tip. A lighted match is held less than an inch beneath this hollow for a few seconds to burn away any of the waxy coating that is often put on foil. While the match is burning, observe if there are any pinholes in the foil. If there are you will see the flame through them. Do not use foil that has any punctures or the molten cocaine may go through them. Do not leave the match under the foil long enough for the metal to glow. Pour the equiva-

lent of a line of cocaine into the hollow. Place a piece
of tubing five or six inches long and ½ inch or more in
diameter in the mouth. A conical device is excellent if
the small end is held in the mouth. The large end will
capture nearly all of the fumes and avoid waste. Exhale completely. Hold a lighted match beneath the
hollow in the foil. The cocaine will quickly melt and
begin to vaporize. Immediately commence inhaling
the vapors. If they are being produced faster than you
can inhale them, remove the match for a moment
while continuing to inhale. Be careful not to let the
flame too near the fumes. They are combustible and
can sear your mouth or lungs.

Sometimes cocaine is diluted in warm vodka and
sprayed onto marijuana or tobacco. After drying it can
be smoked in any manner. Because it does not decom-

pose as easily as the hydrochloride, free-base cocaine is better for smoking.

INJECTION

Intravenous injection is the most efficient way of taking cocaine. The rush is overwhelming and occurs almost instantly. Nevertheless, it is not at all recommended. Even among the most hard-core coke fans, the use of the needle is rare and usually frowned upon. For one thing, it is difficult to determine the correct dose, especially with illicit street cocaine with its unknown cuts. An accidental overdose may have serious results, including respiratory collapse and cardiac arrest.

The usual dose for injection is about ¼ that for snorting; that is, about half a line. Among the possible side effects from intravenously injecting even pure pharmaceutical cocaine are systemic shock, rapid heart palpitations, heavy perspiration, dizziness and nausea. There is also the risk of infection from improperly sterilized equipment.

One of the greatest dangers is that some cuts are poorly soluble and may form emboli or blood clots. Emboli are clots of poorly-soluble material which lodge in the arterioles and capillary beds and obstruct the flow of blood. When the tissues fail to get sufficient oxygen from blood circulation, necrosis and fibrosis may result. Emboli can do serious injury to various organs. Frequently they lodge in the lungs or eyes and lead to respiratory failure or blindness. Talc and benzocaine are dangerous in this respect.

Although the effects of injected cocaine are far more intense than those obtained from snorting it, they are also much shorter-lasting. The peak of stimulation begins to subside after about ten minutes. Residual stimulation dissipates after 30 minutes.

Intramuscular injection is less effective and less dangerous because the drug is absorbed more slowly. The risk of blood clots is eliminated, but the danger of infection still exists. Since the intramuscular route is not much more efficient than snorting, it seems pointless to take the gamble.

SELECTION OF QUALITY
Cuts and Tests

CUTTING COCAINE

The only reason for cutting cocaine is to make more money by cheating the customer. Some dealers will attempt to justify this practice as ethical on the grounds that pure unbuffed cocaine is too strong and, if used repeatedly, can damage the mucous membranes. Perhaps there is a vague fragment of truth in this. If you have absolutely pure cocaine and intend to use it immoderately, it is prudent to buff it first with 20% of some inert and readily absorbed substance such as mannite or inositol. However, the "ethical" dealers of which we speak purchase cocaine that has already been cut to 50% and, in the name of protecting the nasal passages of their beloved customers, cut it further to 25–30%.

Some of the cuts described in this book are relatively harmless; others are not. The author wishes to make it clear that he abhors the use of adulterants in cocaine—or in just about anything. By writing this chapter on cuts he is doubtlessly divulging to unscrupulous dealers many new possible ways to dilute the product and cheat the customer. His purpose is not to provide dealers with a guidebook to that end. He strives instead to give to the customer and to the concerned, well-intentioned middleman adequate information with which to identify the cut and to understand its characteristics and drawbacks well enough to make a sound decision before investing in a product offered for sale. It is also his hope that he will impart some pertinent facts to that large number of dealers whose fault was never a lack of concern, but rather a simple ignorance of what they were doing by employing adulterants. If the difficulty of supporting themselves and their families during these trying times impels them to continue to practice the dubious art of stepping on coke, perhaps through this chapter they will learn of some safer and more preferable adulterants with which to cheat their friends.

In this chapter we will examine each of the standard adulterants used to cut cocaine. We will also examine several which, though not standard, are being seen more and more on the market and which have some qualifications which may make them more common in the future. Under each substance we will consider its virtues and drawbacks as a cut, its effects upon the consumer, its chemical properties, and other points of interest. In the next chapter various tests are given for detecting the presence of a specific adulterant. Several tests are also included for determining the presence of cocaine and for making a rough estimate of its purity.

TYPES OF ADULTERANTS

There are three types of substances used to cut cocaine:

1) **The active cut:** a substance that has some of the stimulating or mood-altering properties of cocaine, but is far less expensive.

2) **The anesthetic cut:** a substance that produces the local numbing effect of cocaine, thus giving the immediate impression of being the real thing.

3) **The inert cut:** a substance that has the appearance of cocaine, but neither numbs nor stimulates.

Whatever category a cut belongs to, it should meet the following primary qualifications:

a) Visual similarity to cocaine. White, preferably with a sparkling, crystalline appearance.

b) No obvious taste or odor.

c) Non-irritating to the mucous membranes, or no more so than cocaine.

d) Non-toxic; causing no undesirable side effects, or none significantly more than cocaine.

It is also preferred that a cut be readily absorbed by the mucous membranes and not clog the nostrils. Not all standard cuts fully meet all these specifications, but the success of any cut is governed by how nearly it does so.

For the most part a cut that fulfills these qualifications will not be readily detectable except by a chemical test or the use of highly sophisticated equipment, such as the gas chromatograph or mass spectrometer. Nevertheless, with relatively simple "in the kitchen" tests we can detect the presence of some adulterants, or at least establish that the sample contains one of several possible substances, all of which have similar properties. For example, an easy-to-perform color reaction test can indicate the presence of one of the cocaine-related anesthetic adulterants, such as procaine, benzocaine or tetracaine, but will not positively show which one it is. Other slightly more involved tests that will pinpoint the adulterant material more precisely are given in this book, but in all cases we have avoided test methods which require special laboratory equipment or excessively complicated procedures.

ACTIVE CUTS

Because of cocaine's unusually high price on the underground market, it is frequently adulterated with one of the less costly and often more potent (milligram for milligram) stimulant or psychoactive materials. Methedrine is probably the cut most frequently used. Many users are so accustomed to snorting cocaine cut with methedrine that when they try pure cocaine they complain that they have been cheated with badly diluted merchandise.

Other active cuts that are less often encountered include PCP and pemoline. Butacaine sulfate is sometimes used as a cocaine adulterant. Unlike the other synthetic -caine drugs, it has stimulating properties like those of cocaine. For this reason it may be regarded as an active cut. But since it is also an anesthetic cut we have placed it under that heading.

Methedrine

Methedrine, sometimes known as Desoxyn, commonly known as speed, and properly called methamphetamine hydrochloride or, more accurately, (+)-2-methylaminopropylbenzene hydrochloride, occurs as odorless, bitter-tasting, fine white crystals or crystalline powder. Like any of the amphetamines, it is a powerful stimulant of the central nervous system, sympathetic nervous system and cerebral centers. It also acts upon some of the metabolic processes. Because of its appearance and stimulant properties it is often used as a cocaine cut. Also, its flame/foil test results are quite similar to those of cocaine. The naive cocaine user cannot usually distinguish the effects of methedrine from those of cocaine. It produces stimulation, alertness and euphoria, but these last longer than those of cocaine. Some of its side effects are much like those of cocaine. These are, for example: drying of the mucous membranes, suppression of appetite and the laxative effect, but these are usually more severe and longer-lasting with methedrine than with cocaine. Some of the characteristics of methedrine which distinguish it from cocaine are: tight feeling in the neck and facial muscles (especially the jaw), sharply bitter taste, and intense smarting of the nasal membranes upon snorting. Moderate use of amphetamines as prescribed by doctors is not particularly dangerous. The amounts used to cut cocaine are not likely to present any danger, if the coke is used moderately. If the coke is used to excess, the risks of the concomitant methedrine also increase. Unlike cocaine, tolerance to methedrine can develop. This is not too likely to occur with meth-cut coke unless one is using large quantities of the mixture daily. Some of the unpleasant effects of cocaine abuse may be accentuated if methedrine is present. These include: dizziness, anxiety, aggressive behavior, insomnia, cardiac stress and palpitations of the heart. There is also a tendency to experience paranoia with extended and excessive use of methedrine.

Pemoline

Pemoline, properly known as 2-imino-5-phenyl-4-oxazolidinone, is a synthetically prepared hydantoin group chemical which was used as a stimulant by American and British flyers on long bombing missions during World War II. It is a fine, shiny, white crystalline powder with a silky, almost greasy feeling when rubbed between the fingers. 20–50 mg orally produces mental stimulation, with some central nervous system stimulation after 30–60 minutes, lasting 6–12 hours. It lacks the unpleasant and dangerous side effects of the amphetamines, such as cardiac stress, drying of the mucous membranes, tension in the neck and facial muscles, rapid development of tolerance, and possible addiction. The aqua-magnesium complex of pemoline, known as magnesium pemoline, has been developed by Abbot Laboratories as an aid to learning and memory function.

Pemoline is fairly new to the list of cuts for cocaine. Its use is still relatively rare, but it is being confronted more and more. It is available on the underground market for $20–$30 per gram and is even less expensive when purchased from legitimate chemical companies. The difficulty in obtaining it, however, is that the Federal Drug Enforcement Agency has issued directives to chemical companies instructing them not to sell this and other chemicals to individuals (only to organizations), and to report the names of people who place such orders. There is no law against pemoline, but the probability is that harassment techniques will be used against the purchaser.

The shiny, crystalline appearance of pemoline blends well with cocaine and adds sparkle to it. It is absorbed through the mucous membranes more slowly than cocaine or the other common psychoactive cuts such as the amphetamines. But after it has been absorbed (15–30 minutes) it produces mental stimulation and alertness that could pass for a cocaine high. It also lengthens the duration of the high because its effects are dispelled 3–4 times more slowly than those of cocaine. Doses of pemoline larger than 20–50 mg prolong all of the effects of the drug, including its insomnia-inducing properties. 250–500 mg of pemoline can keep a person from sleeping for 24–36 hours. This presents a drawback if a person is using cocaine that is heavily cut with pemoline. He will be unable to sleep long after the cocaine high has faded. It is important that a person get adequate rest after using a lot of cocaine. Too much pemoline prevents one from getting this rest, and it may be necessary to resort to sedatives. For this reason, no more than 20% pemoline should be combined with cocaine, generally. On the other hand, a small amount of pemoline mixed with a moderate dose of cocaine can be an excellent drug combination when strong mental alertness is

needed. About 50 mg of cocaine with 20 mg of pemoline is the average individual dose if only one dose is
taken. If the pemoline is taken first, and the cocaine is
taken when the pemoline's initial effects are felt, both
drugs should wear off at about the same time. If
booster doses of cocaine are taken later, they should
not contain any pemoline lest it cause insomnia.
Pemoline is tasteless and causes no irritation to the
nostrils.

PCP

PCP is correctly known as phencyclidine hydrochloride, sometimes bears the trade name Sernyl, and
is popularly called angel dust. The product is often
sold on the underground market because of its peculiar
effects upon the mind and body. It is often combined
with LSD and passed off as psilocybin. It produces an
extreme relaxation of the mind and body which might
better be described as limpness. It has also won some
popularity as a sex drug because it has much the same
inhibition-retarding influence as methaqualone.
Medically it has been reported to produce a variety of
schizoid states, such as body image changes, and to
intensify schizophrenia. It does not tend to produce
hallucinations, however. It was developed as a sensory blocking agent or anesthetic, but its use on
human patients has been abandoned because of its
psychotomimetic effects and prolonged recovery
time. Underground users of PCP and observers have
reported that frequent use of the drug can lead to
mental debility in many individuals. Its pharmacological action is not completely understood, but it has

been suggested that its mechanism may be through direct action on the cortex or by a defect in proprioceptive feedback. About 1% of the street samples of cocaine analyzed by Pharm-Chem Laboratories of Palo Alto, California have been found to contain phencyclidine.

Yohimbine

Yohimbine hydrochloride is an indole-based alkaloid derived from yohimbe, the inner bark of the tropical West African tree *Corynanthe yohimbe*. Its chemical formula is $C_{21}H_{26}O_3N_2 \cdot HCl$. It comes as a fluffy white powder (sometimes yellowish) with very little taste. It is occasionally sold on the underground market because of its psychoactive and aphrodisiac properties.

When 15–50 mg of yohimbine hydrochloride is snorted, it does not produce a reaction as rapidly as cocaine. But after 5 minutes its effects gradually begin to appear. These may include subtle mental and perceptual changes, stimulation, and warm shivers. If the body is tired or run-down, these shivers may be cold. Its effects usually last 2–4 hours, gradually diminishing. Taken orally, its effects are slower to appear (15–30 minutes). It also acts as an aphrodisiac by inhibiting serotonin levels in the brain, by stimulating the spinal ganglia which affect erection, and by bringing increased blood to the genital zone. The warm shivers experienced under yohimbine are enjoyable during intercourse and may give the illusion of bodies melting into one another.

The drawbacks of yohimbine as a coke cut are several. Its dull, fluffy appearance is quite dissimilar to that of cocaine. Pharmacologically it combines badly with some other drugs including alcohol and the amphetamines. Alcohol and yohimbine potentiate each other. If one is using cocaine that has been heavily cut with yohimbine while drinking a lot of liquor, it can be dangerous. If the cocaine has been cut with both yohimbine and an amphetamine, the combination is likely to produce violent, uncontrollable shivers, steep drop in blood pressure, rapid flutter of the heart and pulse, and breathing difficulties with chest pain during inhalation. Persons with an active kidney ailment or any liver disorder should avoid yohimbine, as it may antagonize these conditions.

Yohimbine is legal, but because of recent DEA directives it is difficult to obtain from legitimate chemical companies. It is sometimes sold on the underground market for $25–$35 per gram. It is much cheaper if it can be purchased from a chemical company.

ANESTHETIC CUTS

The anesthetic cuts are often sought after by dealers because, instead of diluting the numbing effect of cocaine, they hasten, intensify and prolong it. Most of them belong to the same chemical group as cocaine and are referred to as synthetic -caine drugs or synthetic benzoic esters. (Lidocaine is an exception, being classified as a xylidide.) They are rapid-acting local anesthetics of short duration. Initial effects wear off within one or two hours. Butacaine is unique in that it also produces central stimulation and euphoria.

There are about 200 synthetic -caine drugs, and almost any of them could be used to cut cocaine. However, the only ones that are likely to be encountered are procaine, lidocaine, benzocaine, tetracaine and butacaine.

All of the -caine drugs affect both the sensory and motor nerves. Because they interrupt nerve transmissions they are classified as toxic agents. High blood levels of these can result in convulsions, respiratory collapse and possible death. This is not a danger when cocaine or any of the -caine drugs are snorted or ingested. The danger is present when large doses are injected intravenously. Intramuscular injection is far safer. Generally these synthetic -caine drugs are safe to use if not injected into the veins. Some individuals may show allergic sensitivity to the -caine drugs no matter how they are administered.

All of the synthetic -caine drugs respond to the bleach test.

Procaine

Procaine Hydrochloride, also known as Novacaine, Allocaine, Biocaine, Clinocaine, Ethocaine, Genocaine and Syncaine, is a synthetic benzoic ester with a salty, slightly bitter taste, and is structurally related to cocaine. Its proper name is diethylaminoethyl-p-aminobenzoate hydrochloride. Its chemical formula is $C_6H_4NH_2COOCH_2CH_2N(C_2H_5)\cdot HCl$. It usually comes as a crystalline powder or as salt-like crystals of even size. Its melting point is 153–156°C. It is soluble in water, in alcohol at 25°C or higher, slightly soluble in chloroform, and nearly insoluble in ether. It is a short-acting local anesthetic, and gives something of

the numbing effect of cocaine. It does not fully penetrate the intact mucous membrane, and is slower to
produce the numbing than many of the other -caine
drugs (2–5 minutes on the tongue). Procaine is a
relatively safe coke cut. It has only ½–⅓ the toxicity
of cocaine. In the system it breaks down into PABA
(one of the B vitamins) and diethylaminoethanol (a
substance normal in our metabolism).

One of the standard tests used by dealers to determine the quality of cocaine is to drop some sample
into a glass of water. If the crystals, as they descend to
the bottom, leave faint transparent trailers behind
them, it is supposed to be pure cocaine hydrochloride.
Pure procaine hydrochloride, however, will do exactly
the same thing. Because procaine hydrochloride
looks, tastes and leaves trailers like cocaine, coke is
often cut with large amounts of it. Sometimes 100%
procaine is sold as cocaine. Since procaine has no
stimulating properties, the duped customer gets no
high unless he is easily swayed by placebos. Sometimes procaine is spiked with amphetamines, LSD or
PCP and sold as cocaine.

Free-base procaine is sometimes used as a cocaine
cut. It usually comes as rather dull white powder. It
lacks the luster of the more preferred coke cuts but is
quicker to cause a numbing effect than the hydrochloride. It is poorly soluble in water and therefore
tends to linger in the nostrils and sometimes prompts
sneezing.

Tetracaine

Tetracaine hydrochloride, correctly known as 2-di-
methyl-aminoethyl-parabutylaminobenzoate   hydro-

chloride, and also known as Pontocaine and Amethocaine, is an odorless, white crystalline powder with a slightly bitter taste. Its chemical formula is $CH_3(CH_2)_3NHC_6H_4COOCH_2CH_2N(CH_3)_2 \cdot HCl$. It is a synthetic benzoic ester and has about the same anesthetic potency as cocaine. Its anesthetic effect lasts longer than procaine. Its toxicity is about 7 times that of procaine or 2–3 times that of cocaine.

Benzocaine

Benzocaine, properly known as ethyl-para-aminobenzoate, comes as white crystals or as a white crystalline powder. It is odorless with a slightly bitter taste. Its chemical formula is $C_6H_4NH_2CO_2C_2H_5$.

Benzocaine is used in 3–5% dilution in dusting powders and anesthetic ointments such as Solarcaine®. It has low toxicity and is considered safe for snorting and ingestion. But because of its poor solubility in water as compared to the other -caine drugs, it is dangerous if injected. It can form emboli, blood clots and other complications. About 3% of the street cocaine samples analyzed by Pharm-Chem Laboratories of Palo Alto, California had been cut with benzocaine.

Butacaine

Butacaine sulfate, properly known as 3-di-n-butyl-amino-propyl-para-aminobenzoate sulfate, and sometimes known as Butyn, is another synthetic benzoic ester chemically related to cocaine. It comes as a dullish white powder. It is soluble in water, acetone and warm alcohol, slightly soluble in chloroform, and insoluble in ether.

As a cocaine cut, it has the advantage of causing a swift numbing effect and some of the stimulating properties of cocaine. Its numbing effect lasts considerably longer than that of cocaine and the other synthetic local anesthetics. It has the disadvantage of being more toxic than cocaine, and sometimes more irritating to the mucous membranes. If too much is snorted it may cause nosebleeds.

Lidocaine

Lidocaine hydrochloride, also known as Lignocaine hydrochloride and xylocaine, is the monohydrate of diethylaminoacet-2,6-xylidide hydrochloride. Its chemical formula is $C_6H_3(CH_3)_2NHCOCH_2N(C_2H_5)_2 \cdot HCl \cdot H_2O$. Although it has anesthetic properties and also responds to the bleach test, it is not a member of the benzoic ester family, but is grouped with the xylidides. It is anesthetically five times as potent as procaine hydrochloride, but is only twice as toxic. This is about the same toxicity as cocaine hydrochloride. It occurs as an odorless, white crystalline powder with a slightly bitter taste. The free base of lidocaine, which is sometimes used as a cocaine cut too, occurs as white to slightly yellow crystals or crystalline powder with a slightly bitter taste and a characteristic odor. Although lidocaine hydrochloride reacts readily to the bleach test (see page 83), free-base lidocaine is so poorly water-soluble that its reaction is extremely slow. After thirty minites in the bleach, it will show hardly any color change. It may take on a slightly yellow tint, unlike the other synthetic -caine drugs, which turn brick-orange almost immediately.

The combination of cocaine hydrochloride and free-base lidocaine, however, does produce a unique reaction in bleach (see 1979 Bleach Test Update, page 85).

INERT CUTS

Little need be said of the inert cuts. They are merely white powdery or crystalline materials used to dilute the product. They add nothing to either the reality or the illusion of the cocaine experience.

Mannite

Mannite (mannitol) is a white, crystalline, hexahydric alcohol found natively in several plants, including the manna ash tree (*Fraxinus ornus*) and the New Zealand plant *Myoporum lactum*. Commercially, however, mannitol is made from the hydrogenation of glucose. The chemical formula of mannitol is $(CH_2OH(CHOH)_4CH_2OH$. It has a slightly sweet taste. Commercially it is used in making resins, plasticisers, pharmaceutical preparations, laxatives, fillers for pills, and as a nutrient. It is available in three forms: powder, granules, and compressed blocks.

The preferred form for cutting cocaine is the softly compressed block of paper-wrapped mannite which is sold in Europe as a baby laxative and nutrient. Fine slivers are easily shaved from the block with a sharp pocket knife, X-acto knife or single-edge razor blade and chopped further to tiny flakes which have the glistening appearance of cocaine. The granule form is also useful as a cut, but is not often available.

The least preferred form is the fine white powder. It lacks the sparkling cocaine-like appearance of the block shavings and the granules. Some dealers use it successfully by employing the following procedure: The powdered mannitol is thoroughly and homogeneously combined with finely pulverized cocaine and spread thinly and evenly on a smooth, non-absorbent surface. The mixture is then lightly and evenly sprayed with water from an atomizer or plant mister and allowed to dry. As the damp mannitol powder dries it will form tiny crystals. The cocaine crystals help to seed the growth of the mannitol crystals. It may have to be sprayed and dried several times to get the crystallization started. For this reason it is best to use distilled water. The impurities in tap water are inclined to discolor the product. This procedure usually takes some practice before the knack is achieved. The purity of the cocaine has much to do with how well this technique works. If the product is already heavily cut there may not be enough cocaine crystals to initiate the mannitol crystallization. The correct amount of moisture is also essential to the success of this process. One must get the material damp, but not soggy. Other factors which may influence the results are the humidity and the temperature. Some people get good results at room temperature. Others find it necessary to dry the product in an oven at a low temperature.

There are several reasons why mannite is one of the most popular cuts for cocaine. It has a good cocaine-like appearance. It is rapidly absorbed by the mucous membranes. Its slight sweetness is barely noticeable when mixed. It is non-toxic, non-irritating and phar-

macologically rather inert. It may cause a slight post-
nasal drip in some individuals, but, because of its
swift assimilation, this does not usually last very long.
Many people report a laxative effect after snorting a
fair amount of cocaine cut with mannitol. If one is
sensitive to mannitol's laxative properties, this can be
a good way of determining its presence, but it should
be remembered that cocaine may also have a mild
laxative effect, as does methedrine, with which it is
sometimes cut.

One of the main reasons that mannitol is used as a
coke cut is that it passes the flame test (see tests).
When pharmaceutical cocaine is heated to disintegra-
tion on a piece of foil, it vaporizes, leaving no residue.
Also, its fumes ignite like those of cocaine. Most of
the standard cuts leave either a charred residue or a
golden-brown stain. It is assumed by many dealers
that all cuts leave some residue or stain and that this is
a sure way to test for purity. This is true only up to a
point, however. Mannitol is one of the few cuts that
evaporate like pharmaceutical cocaine, leaving no
residue whatsoever.

Inositol

Inositol correctly refers to any of a number of similar
chemicals belonging to a group known as hexahy-
droxycyclohexanes. The kind used as a coke cut is
called meso-inositol or myo-inositol. It is also a B
vitamin and is almost totally non-toxic. As much as 40
grams have been consumed in laboratory tests without any ill effects. Only the meso or myo form has
vitamin activity. It is found in yeast, grains, citrus

fruits and meat and is commercially prepared from corn. Its chemical formula is $C_6H_6(OH)_6$. It comes as white crystalline granules with a slightly sweet taste. It is soluble in water and insoluble in absolute alcohol and in ether. It is available in granule form at many health food stores for about $8.00 per 4-ounce jar. Because of its sparkly appearance and non-toxicity it is a rather common cut. It is absorbed fairly well via the mucous membrane, but a little slower than mannitol. Using a lot of inositol-cut coke within a short amount of time may clog the nostrils for a while. Although it is a hexahydric crystalline alcohol like mannitol, it does not have any of the latter substance's laxative effects.

Lactose

Lactose, or milk sugar, because of its low price (about $1.50 per pound) and availability at health food stores and pharmacies, is one of the most common substances used to cut cocaine and other drugs. Its proper chemical name is 4-β-galactopyranosylglucopyranose. Its chemical formula is $C_{12}H_{22}O_{11} \cdot H_2O$. It usually is sold as a white crystalline powder or crystalline mass. It is found in milk and milk products and is commercially derived from whey. It tends to absorb moisture from humid air, causing it to lump. It is odorless and its taste is not quite as sweet as sucrose (cane sugar). It is non-toxic except in some very rare allergy cases such as galactosemia, a genetic disorder in which the body is unable to produce the enzyme, lactase, needed to break down lactose.

Its greatest drawback as a cocaine adulterant lies in the fact that it picks up moisture, but is rather slowly absorbed through the nasal membranes. It tends to clog the nostrils, especially if large amounts are snorted. This clogging is annoying and also wasteful. Cocaine mingled with the lumps of lactose in the nostrils is not absorbed and is frequently sneezed or blown from the nose. Also, any lactose still in the nostrils may act as an obstruction to the absorption of any cocaine snorted on top of it.

Talc

Talc, magnesium trisilicate, is a soft, finely-powdered mineral used as a lubricative and protective skin covering. It is pharmacologically inert and is not absorbed at all through the mucous lining. It is not directly irritating to the mucous membranes, but it will clog the nostrils—especially if a lot is snorted—and may cause sinus difficulties.

The danger of using talc as a coke cut lies in the possibility that it may be injected. Both talc and corn-starch—as well as flour, which is sometimes used—are for the most part insoluble in the blood. After injection they may form blood clots or emboli and lodge in the arterioles and capillary beds, obstructing the flow of blood and causing serious injury and possible death. There have been numerous cases of persons who injected talc-adulterated cocaine and developed emboli in the lungs and eyes leading to respiratory failure and blindness.

Because of its great insolubility, talc is easily removed from cocaine (see section entitled Removal of Cuts).

Cornstarch

Cornstarch, because of its inexpensive price and availability in grocery stores, has occasionally been used as a cocaine adulterant. It is non-toxic and relatively harmless when the cocaine is snorted or ingested, although it tends to clog in the nostrils because of its habit of congealing in the presence of moisture. It is dangerous, however, if injected intravenously because it is likely to form blood clots and emboli.

Quinine

Quinine sulfate is an odorless, bitter-tasting, white crystalline powder derived from cinchona bark. It gained fame at one time for its anti-malarial activity, but has now been replaced for the most part by the synthetic drugs. It reduces body temperature, serves as an analgesic to control mild pain and fever, relaxes skeletal muscles, functions as a sclerosing agent in the treatment of varicose veins, and acts as a smooth muscle relaxant to induce labor and abortion. Its toxic effects include impaired hearing, ringing in the ears, headaches, visual disturbances, nausea, vertigo, and diarrhea. Oral use can provoke gastric disturbances. Intramuscular injection can induce tissue irritation and lesions. Intravenous injection can cause thrombosis of the vein of injection and an alarmingly sharp drop in blood pressure. Heavy poisoning can lead to renal damage, acute hemolytic anemia, and overstimulation of the central nervous system resulting in coma and death due to respiratory arrest. The average lethal dose is 8 grams, but death has been recorded from less than half a gram. There have been numerous reports of quinine adulteration in cocaine, but it is much more commonly used to cut heroin. A large percentage of the recorded heroin overdose deaths are actually due to quinine rather than heroin. Its poor solubility makes it dangerous to inject intravenously.

MISCELLANEOUS CUTS

Other adulterants occasionally used with cocaine include boric acid, H_3BO_3; Epsom salts (magnesium sulfate), $MgSO_4 \cdot 7H_2O$; and baking soda (sodium bicarbonate), $NaHCO_3$. All of these are relatively safe under most circumstances. Mention was made in the article, "A Very Expensive High," by Richard Rhodes (*Playboy*, January 1975) of the use of an amino acid as a cocaine adulterant. The party who introduced Rhodes to cocaine recommended this substance as a coke cut because it adds bulk without any taste or effect. This would be true of almost any amino acid, but no mention was made of which of the many amino acids was used (possibly methionine). White flour sometimes has been employed as a cut, but its tendency to congeal in the presence of moisture gives it the same drawbacks as cornstarch. It is very dangerous if it is injected.

Caffeine is sometimes used as a cut because of its stimulating properties. It is relatively harmless and is absorbed rather poorly. But the effective dose of caffeine is so high (200–500 mg) that it really doesn't add any punch to the product. If anything, it dilutes it. Ephedrine sulfate is a stimulant derived from the ori-

ental Ephedra plant. It is mostly a sympathetic stimulant and moderately a central stimulant. Its effects last
2–4 hours. The effective dose is 25–50 mg. It is generally safe and is used medicinally to induce bronchial
dilation in asthma cases.

TESTING COCAINE

If you have a sample of illicit cocaine and wish to find
out how pure it is and what adulterants have been
added, there are several ways to make a rough determi-
nation. We will consider these in their most probable
order, starting with examination of the sample and
observation of its effects, and progressing through the
most elementary "kitchen" tests to the more accurate
chemical tests for specific adulterants.

The test methods given in this book are for the most
part qualitative—not quantitative. They can tell you
what adulterants have been used, but not how much of
them are present. In some cases, through careful observation, a very rough estimate of the quantity of the
cut may be made. But the only way that reasonably
accurate percentages may be expressed is by use of
rather expensive analytical equipment and highly involved techniques.

Visual Appearance

Many dealers and customers believe that they can
judge the quality of cocaine by its appearance. Although there may be a few things that can be learned
by looking at the product, it is not a very reliable
approach.

Refined cocaine is usually 85 to 92% pure at best, the remainder being other coca alkaloids such as L-ecgonine, benzoyl ecgonine, hygrine, cinnamyl cocaine, and α- and β-truxilline (cocamine). It is likely to come as either rocks or flakes. Whether cocaine is in rock or flake form does not necessarily have any bearing upon its potency. Pharmaceutical cocaine is almost always flake and is at least 99% pure. It does not contain the other coca alkaloids. Whether in rock or flake form, uncut cocaine has a shiny, almost transparent appearance. When pulverized the powder still has a dull sparkle to it. Small samples of cocaine (e.g., grams) usually contain a good percentage of powder. This is partly because it frequently gets crushed in handling, but most often because it is intentionally pulverized in order to add a cut.

The general belief is that rock cocaine is free of adulterants. Many dealers make something of a ritual of showing these rocks to their customers, carefully slicing a rock with a razor blade to reveal its crystalline layers. This is no guarantee of purity, however. Often a dealer will reconstitute powdered cocaine to rocks or flakes after adding a cut.

Some cuts, such as procaine hydrochloride, boric acid, shaved block mannite, inositol and methedrine, are quite similar to cocaine in appearance and can be added to flake cocaine and not be detected visually. Other cuts, like quinine sulfate and Epsom salts, are somewhat less shiny than cocaine, but are still difficult to spot with the naked eye. Some cuts, such as dextrose and lactose, have a much duller appearance than cocaine and may be detected if enough has been added.

In brief, there is little that can be judged by visually inspecting cocaine. It is worthwhile, however, to take a look at your sample for what it might show before going on to more revealing methods of examination.

Taste Test

Pure cocaine has a slightly bitter, medicinal flavor. Some cuts may alter the taste somewhat. Dextrose sweetens the product. So does lactose, but less so than dextrose. Inositol and mannitol both have a sweetish taste and, if enough has been added, may sweeten the cocaine, or at least lessen some of its bitterness. Synthetic -caine drugs are bitter like cocaine. Their hydrochlorides are both bitter and salty. The synthetic -caine drugs will numb the tongue more swiftly than cocaine, and their anesthetic effect will last longer. On the other hand, inert cuts will dilute and alter the slight and brief numbing effect of the cocaine. Because some people are aware of these facts, many dealers will balance their cuts. For example—add a little mannite or other inert cut which dilutes the numbing properties of the cocaine, and a little procaine to return its anesthetic potency back to that of pure cocaine.

The purity of cocaine can be judged by placing a large flake, crystal or rock fragment of the sample between the tip of the tongue and the roof of the mouth. If the cocaine melts in the mouth like butter and leaves no gritty residue, it is likely to be quite pure. If the product has been reconstituted with an adulterant such as mannite (which also melts in the mouth), the sweetness of that cut should be detectable.

Snort Test

While visual examination tells little if anything about
the quality of cocaine, and tasting shows possibly a
little more, actually snorting the coke is probably the
most revealing of the direct sensory tests which do not
require some special procedure such as weighing,
measuring, burning or chemical reaction. The most
significant test of illicit cocaine must inevitably be:
does it do for you what cocaine is supposed to do?
Does it feel like cocaine? Does it give you the increased energy, mental clarity and euphoric feeling
that may be expected from cocaine? The validity of
such a test, of course, is greatly dependent upon one's
sophistication with the drug. The precise effects of
cocaine may often be influenced by the state of mind
and metabolism at the time of using it. Whether one is
tired or wired, hungry or hung-over, etc., can make a
difference. Therefore one must have had some experience with cocaine under these various circumstances
to make a sound judgment.

The first thing that may be observed upon snorting
a sample of cocaine is how it feels as it hits the nasal
passages. If it burns more than coke usually does and
brings tears to the eyes, it may contain some methedrine. Bear in mind, however, that even pure cocaine
does this to most novices and even to veteran snorters
if their membranes are sensitive at the time. If the
coke has a sharply bitter taste, there is further evidence that methedrine may be present. If there is a
laxative effect after several hours, this may be further
evidence that the sample contains methedrine. It
should be remembered, however, that mannitol,

Epsom salts and cocaine itself may also act as laxatives, although to a lesser degree than methedrine.

In less than a minute after snorting you should notice the medicinal aftertaste in the back of the throat. This is the taste and odor of cocaine. If it is missing or heavily obscured by other tastes, you should begin to harbor some doubts about the sample. After a few minutes the anesthetic properties of the drug may be felt as a numbing or "freeze" effect in the upper nostrils and frontal upper gums. If this is felt more intensely than normal for pure cocaine, it is probable that a synthetic -caine drug has been added. If the "freeze" persists for more than 30 minutes, there is almost no doubt that this is the case. You may not notice the "freeze" so much by this time because you may have become used to it. But if you clack your teeth together, you can feel whether they are numb or not. Around this time one may also experience a pronounced post-nasal drip. If this is the case, it is possible that the cocaine has been cut with either lactose, mannite or Epsom salts.

It may be difficult at first to tell whether the stimulating effects of a sample are purely those of cocaine or if they are due to the presence of some other stimulant such as methedrine, pemoline or yohimbine. One must have had some experience with these drugs, as well as with cocaine, to make a valid judgment. Usually methedrine makes one feel more wired than cocaine. However, this is not always a reliable indication. Cocaine may wire a person more than usual if his mood and metabolism are so predisposed at the time. Other indications of the presence of methedrine are a drying of the mucuous membranes of the nose and mouth and a tight feeling in the jaw, which should commence 30–60 minutes after snorting and may persist for several hours. Cocaine may also cause a drying of the membranes, but not as severely as methedrine, and without the tight jaw effect. If pemoline has been added to the cocaine, you will probably notice a second wave of stimulation 45–60 minutes after snorting, as that slow-acting drug begins to take effect. If, two hours after snorting a couple of lines, the user feels far more active than he usually would from coke and does not feel like he is mellowing out, it is probable that the sample has been cut with some longer-acting stimulant. If there is an extended period of stimulation and a sufficient number of the indications of amphetamine have been noted (i.e., bitter taste, smarting at first and later drying out of the nostrils, tight jaw, wired feeling and laxative effect), it is quite apparent that the sample contains one of these drugs. If stimulation persists, but those other indications are absent, it is likely that another CNS stimulant has been added. It should be remembered, however, that if the sample has been cut with methedrine and also contains sugar, the bitter taste will be reduced. If mannite or Epsom salts are present, they may cause moisture to be drawn to the surface of the tissues of the nose and throat and thereby counter the drying effect of the methedrine. If a synthetic local anesthetic has been added, it may ameliorate the stinging effect of the methedrine.

Trail Test

A common test employed by many dealers to determine the purity of cocaine involves sprinkling a small

quantity of the sample on the surface of water in a clear drinking glass. Supposedly, if, and only if, it is cocaine, each particle will have a thin transparent trail following it as it sinks to the bottom. Using this test, a dealer will make a quantitative judgment. The estimated percentage of particles which have trails is compared with the percentage which do not. Unfortunately, this is not a fully reliable test. Procaine hydrochloride also produces trails as it sinks. A correction for this discrepancy is given in the Bleach Test (below).

Bleach Test

This simple test detects the presence of any of the synthetic anesthetics — procaine, lidocaine, butacaine, benzocaine, tetracaine, etc. To conduct it, fill a clear drinking glass with a liquid laundry bleach (Clorox®, Purex®, etc.). Sprinkle a small amount of the sample on the surface of the bleach-water. As it submerges in the liquid, any synthetic anesthetic will turn rust-orange. Hydrochlorides and other water-soluble salts of these anesthetics will submerge rapidly, turn deep rust immediately, and leave pale milky-rust trails behind the descending particles. Submerging cocaine particles will be followed by milky-white trails, and an oil-like slick will remain on the surface. Free-base synthetic anesthetics will disperse on the surface and remain there for a long while. After about one minute the material will begin to develop a tint of rust. As the color deepens, some particles will sink. These are seen as slowly descending milky-rust trails. A rough quantitative estimate can be made by carefully observing the proportion of cocaine trails. When free-base anesthetics combined with coke are tested in bleach, descending cocaine particles can drag anesthetic particles downward with them. To the unpracticed eye these may appear to be hydrochlorides, but their descent is slower than the latter's.

There are several street myths regarding the bleach test which, unfortunately, have found their way into print. One is that methedrine and other amphetamines will submerge as pink trails. Another is that quinine sulfate will fizz or burst violently on the surface, then come together as a red dot. Actually, methedrine will dissolve as a white oily solution, leaving a white oily precipitate on the bottom. Dexedrine (d-amphetamine sulfate) reacts almost the same as cocaine; that is, white trails and oily slick. Quinine sulfate disperses rapidly on the surface and remains there. A few particles may sink but will not dissolve. There is no bursting, no fizzing, and no red dot.

The reaction (or lack of reaction) of quinine is so similar to that of heroin that the mythical red dot test can be dangerously misleading. Quinine is often used as a heroin cut and has been correctly blamed for most of the so-called "heroin overdose" deaths. A cautious heroin user who employs this test will witness no red dot reaction, and will be deceived into thinking that there is no quinine present.

Some testers use the bleach test to detect the presence of other cuts. Mannitol, they observe, drops to the bottom and remains there, lactose sinks quickly and lays on the bottom in tiny grains, and inositol descends as particles that glisten like raindrops, etc.

While it is true that these substances will behave as described, so will thousands of other chemicals. Because these are such common cuts, chances are fair that the material is one of these, but there is no assurance that it is. The test only suggests what a substance may be. Further, more determinate testing is recommended. All that the bleach test can really determine is whether or not there is a synthetic -caine drug present and whether it exists as a free base or a salt.

1979 Bleach Test Update

An article titled "The Great Cocaine Clorox Test Controversy" was published in the November 1977 issue of *Head Magazine*. The article presented the conflicting views of myself and of David Lee, author of *The Cocaine Consumer's Handbook* (And/Or Press, 1976), regarding the uses and results of the bleach test. My statement, supported by studies conducted by Pharm-Chem Laboratories of Palo Alto, California, and by Dr. Ronald K. Siegel of UCLA, was—as mentioned above—that amphetamines did not produce pink trails and that quinine did not burst, fizz and produce a red dot on the bleach surface. Lee insisted that these reactions did take place, and, to lend credence to his opinion, he presented photographs showing what he claimed was quinine-cut bursting, fizzing, and forming a red dot.

Although it had been thoroughly proven that quinine by itself does not react to the bleach test, I felt that a reasonable question remained: would a mixture of cocaine and quinine in bleach result in a three-way reaction and produce Lee's fizzing and red dot? In

conducting experimental research for my own book,
I was handicapped by the difficulty or impossibility
of obtaining pure samples of cocaine and other controlled substances. Most of my tests had been done
with pure samples of the various cuts, not mixed with
cocaine. Again I requested Dr. Siegel, who is licensed
to handle controlled drugs, to repeat his experiments
with the bleach test, this time using mixtures of the
cuts with cocaine. The results of his experiments
were most revealing and have forever resolved the
controversy.

Quinine mixed with cocaine does not fizz or form a
red dot. The cocaine descends, producing its characteristic milky-white trails, while the quinine remains
floating on the surface. But when a mixture of cocaine
hydrochloride and free-base lidocaine was tested,
there was a violent bursting and fizzing on the surface
of the bleach, and a few minutes later, a red dot ap-
peared. This was the same reaction that Lee, and
others before him, had attributed to quinine, and
which Lee had unwittingly displayed in his photographs. In fairness to David Lee, I should point out
that the quinine/bleach red dot reaction has been a
long-standing street myth. He did not start it, but
merely perpetuated it.

Free-base lidocaine by itself does not react in this
manner. It floats on the surface, fails to dissolve, produces a slight, yellowish color change, only after
thirty minutes or more. It is only when cocaine is also
present that the dramatic reaction takes place.

If the reader wants further information on the
Bleach Test Controversy, including copies of the arti-

cle and letters published in *Head*, please send 50¢ to Twentieth Century Alchemist, P.O. Box 3684, Manhattan Beach, CA 90266. Request TCA Bulletin #5.

Solvent Test

This test is based upon the fact that cocaine is soluble in certain solvents in which some of the common adulterants are not. For example, cocaine is soluble in chloroform, whereas lactose, dextrose, and inositol are not. If coke is suspected of containing any of these adulterants, it is weighed and then dissolved in chloroform, and the solution passed through a filter paper. The chloroform-insoluble cuts will be left behind in the filter. The chloroform, which contains the cocaine alkaloids and possibly other chloroform-soluble cuts, is then evaporated in a water bath, and the remaining crystals are weighed and compared with the original weighing. If 10 grams of coke weigh 7 grams after going through this process, it was apparently cut with 30% chloroform-insoluble substances. Detailed instructions for carrying out this procedure are given in the following chapter. Other cuts can be similarly removed if a solvent of cocaine can be found which is not a solvent for the cut.

A reverse to the above procedure may also be conducted. If there is a solvent in which cocaine will not dissolve, but a suspected cut will, the coke is dissolved in this solvent and filtered. The liquids which pass through the filter will contain only the cut, but the cocaine will still be in the filter. It can then be washed through the filter with methanol and evaporated down to the purified crystals. If weighing is done before and after, the percentage of the cut can be determined.

Test Kits

Western Scientific Products produces kits for testing various drugs. One kit tests for the presence of cocaine. By carefully observing the degree of color reaction, one can make a rough estimate of the percentage of cocaine present. Another kit can be used to detect the presence of amphetamines. These kits cost about $5 each. Complete instructions are included with each kit.

Flame/Foil Tests

When pure pharmaceutical cocaine is placed on a piece of aluminum foil and a flame is held beneath the foil, the cocaine melts and vaporizes, leaving virtually no residue upon the foil. If the product is a refined mixed-alkaloid cocaine rather than pharmaceutical cocaine, it will leave a reddish-brown stain and a bit of residue on the foil. This is because of the other coca alkaloids (cocamine, hygrine, ecgonine, benzoyl-ecgonine, etc.) that are part of refined cocaine. Some of the common cuts leave a more prominent residue or behave in a specific manner during decomposition. The following is a guide to the Flame/Foil Test characteristics of some of the common cuts.

Mannitol: Melts and evaporates with little visible fumes and leaves no residue.

Inositol: Melts, then burns or decomposes to a black ash.

Lactose: Bubbles, caramelizes, and decomposes to a black ash, while producing a sweetish-smelling smoke like the odor of toasting marshmallows.

Dextrose: Same responses as lactose.

Pemoline: Melts, produces white fumes with burning plastic odor and leaves golden-brown stain.

Procaine hydrochloride: Melts, producing much white fumes with mild chlorine odor. The molten mass turns yellow, progresses to dark gold and leaves a golden-brown stain.

Procaine (free base): Melts quickly with little visible fumes and leaves no residue.

Butacaine sulfate: Decomposes with much fumes and a faint burning rubber or gunpowder odor and leaves a thick black ash.

Methedrine: Melts and vaporizes much like cocaine, but sizzles and pops. Leaves no residue.

Yohimbine hydrochloride: Melts, producing heavy white fumes with indole odor (a fetid odor with a slight pungency like moth flakes). The molten mass turns golden-brown and disappears, leaving a black stain.

Talc: Does not melt, vaporize or decompose.

Baking soda: Does not melt, vaporize or decompose.

Boric acid: After somewhat more heating than is required to decompose cocaine and most other cuts, it will bubble and fuse to a solid lump, but not decompose.

Epsom salts: Does not melt, vaporize or decompose.

When a lighted match is applied to cocaine fumes, they will ignite. This test is sometimes used to determine the purity of the product. Actually it proves very little. Coke fumes will ignite readily unless the product has been very heavily cut. Also, several adulterants, such as mannitol and procaine, will ignite like cocaine.

Melting Point Test

Further verification of the identity of a substance can be made by employing this method. Cocaine and each substance used to adulterate it melt or decompose within a particular temperature range, or in some cases do not melt at all. Pure cocaine hydrochloride will melt somewhere between 192° and 197°C. The extent of the product's impurity can be observed by the degree to which there is a deviation from this range in the melt test. To some extent, the identity of the adulterant may be determined by observing the melting properties of the sample. If the adulterant can be separated from the product by solvent extraction (see Improvement of Cocaine), the identity of the substance can be easily verified by the melting point test. It is necessary to conduct the test with precision in order to obtain accurate results. For the bath fluid, use clear silicone oil having a viscosity of 500–100 centistokes at normal temperature. Use a melt point thermometer with an immersion line. These are graded for different temperature ranges: type 1 for temperatures below 50°C, type 2 for 50°–100°C, type 3 for 100°– 150°C, type 4 for 150°–200°C, type 5 for 200°–250°C, type 6 for 250°–320°C. Use a hard glass capillary tube 120 mm long, 0.8–1.2 mm inner diameter, walls 0.2– 0.3 mm thick, and closed at one end.

Reduce the sample to a fine powder. Dry it in a desiccator over silica gel for 24 hours to remove residual
moisture. Place the sample in a dried capillary tube
and pack the powder tightly in a layer 2.5–3.5 mm
high by dropping it repeatedly through a glass tube
about 700 mm long held vertically over a watch glass.
Select a thermometer which has a range that includes
the melting point of the substance which you suspect
the sample to be. Heat the bath fluid until the temperature rises to about 10° less than the expected melting
point. Place the immersion line of the thermometer at
a level with the meniscus of the bath. Insert the capillary tube into the coil spring so that the material is
level with the mercury bulb of the thermometer. Continue heating so that the temperature rises about 3°
per minute until it reaches 5° below the expected
melting point. Then regulate the rate to 1° per minute.
Watch the indication on the thermometer and note at
what temperature the material in the capillary tube
liquefies completely, leaving no visible solid traces.
Compare the melting point of the material with the
melting points given below. If the material fails to
melt, raise the temperature until it does so. Change to
a higher-range thermometer if necessary.

Cocaine hydrochloride: 192°–197°C
Cocaine (free base): 96°–98°C
Procaine hydrochloride: 153°–156°C
Procaine (free base): 60°C
Tetracaine hydrochloride: 147°–150°C
Benzocaine: 88°–90°C
Butacaine sulfate: 100°–103°C
Lidocaine hydrochloride: 76°–79°C

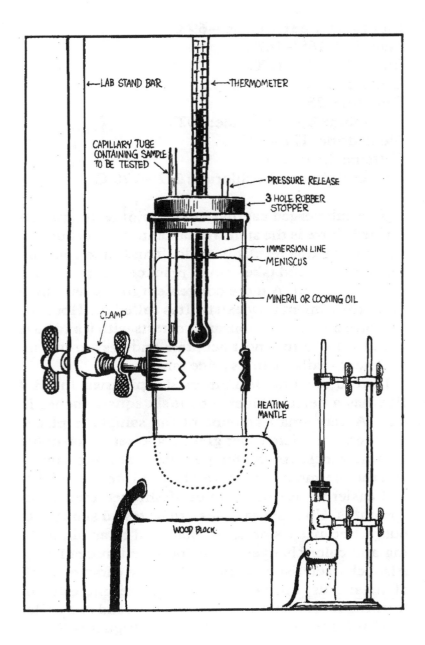

Lidocaine (free base): 66°–69°C
Mannitol: 165°–167°C
Inositol: 224°–227°C
Lactose: 203.5°C (decomp.)
Pemoline: 259°C
Yohimbine hydrochloride: 302°C
Methedrine: 171°–175°C
Caffeine: 235°–237°C
Phencyclidine hydrochloride: 222°–228°C

The submerged capillary melt point technique described above is the standard laboratory procedure for
conducting this test. It is difficult and time-consuming to set up, and takes much practice before one can
carry it off well. A more convenient instrument melt
point instrument now exists. It is called the Hot Box.
We have conducted thousands of tests with it and have
found it to be the most accurate and easy-to-use instrument available in its price range.

Instead of using oil-immersed capillaries, the Hot
Box has a heating block, about six square inches in
size. A very small amount of the sample is placed
between two micro cover glasses and set on top of the
heating block. As the temperature rises, the sample
and the thermometer are watched. It is much quicker
and easier to use than the old-fashioned melt point
apparatus. Up to six samples can be tested simultane-
ously. Because vision is not obscured by an oil, melting and color changes can be observed more clearly.
Also, characteristic odors, such as the caramel smell
of sugar cuts, can be noted. If you are interested in
learning more about this instrument, send one dollar
to Third Eye Instruments, 155 West Figueroa Street,

Santa Barbara, CA 93101. They will send you a bro-
chure describing the Hot Box and their 28 page in-
struction booklet, so that you can familiarize yourself
with the instrument and its operation before making
your decision to purchase one.

Standard Chemical Tests

The following are standard tests for identifying specific substances which are likely to be used as adulterants in cocaine. Tests for identifying cocaine are also
given. Each test or group of tests is presented under
the name of the substance for which the test is intended. These names are not in alphabetical order,
but related substances tend to be grouped together. In
some cases more than one test method is given. Where
this is so, it is recommended that all available tests be
conducted on the material for thorough verification.

Most of these tests are intended for the identifica-
tion of a more or less pure sample of the material for
which the test is designed. In some instances it may be
necessary to use a larger amount of the cocaine sample containing the suspected material. That is, if the
test calls for a 2.5% solution of a material suspected to
be lidocaine hydrochloride and you believe that your
cocaine sample may contain a probable amount of this
cut (say 20–25%), then you may need to use, instead,
4–5 times the amount of sample material called for in
the test (10–12.5% solution). If the adulterant first has
been separated from the cocaine sample by means of
the solvent extraction methods described in the following chapter and the filter residue or the solvent
containing the adulterant is dried by evaporation, the

remaining material may probably be regarded as pure enough to be employed in the test in the amount suggested here. In this case no compensation need be made unless it is believed that other substances of the same solubility or insolubility may also be present.

In some cases it would be impossible to dissolve the recalculated amount of the sample in the quantity of solvent called for in the test. In such an instance, if the amount of sample suggested in test is used, the color reaction may still take place, but the results may be less intense. That is, if the positive reaction is that the solution turns red, it may only turn pink if the sample contains only 20% of the adulterant for which the test is designed. Although the tests given here are qualitative and not quantitative, with some experience the tester may learn to make rough quantitative estimates by the degree of the reaction.

Butacaine sulfate (method 1): To an aqueous solution of the material add sodium hydroxide solution. A colorless oil precipitates.

Butacaine sulfate (method 2): Three-part test. All three must prove positive. Prepare a solution of the material in water, 100 mg/ml. Divide in three portions. (a) To one portion add potassium mercuriiodide solution. A white precipitate occurs. (b) To another portion add iodine solution. A brown precipitate occurs. (c) To another portion add trinitrophenol solution. A yellow precipitate occurs.

Benzocaine: Dissolve 10 mg of the material in 1 ml of water containing 1 drop of dilute hydrochloric acid. Add 2 drops of 10% sodium nitrite solution and 2 drops of a solution consisting of 10 mg of beta-napthol in 5 ml of sodium hydroxide solution. If the material is benzocaine, the solution will turn deep red. If allowed to stand for a while, a scarlet precipitate will form.

Tetracaine hydrochloride: Dissolve about 100 mg of the material in 10 ml of water. Add 0.2 ml dilute hydrochloric acid and 0.2 ml of 10% sodium nitrite solution to it. Add this solution slowly to 2 ml of beta-naphthol solution. If the material is tetracaine hydrochloride, no color will appear, but a white precipitate will form.

Procaine hydrochloride (method 1): Combine equal parts of a 10% solution of the material and a 5% solution of sodium hydroxide. If the material is procaine hydrochloride, it will form a colorless, oily precipitate. If allowed to stand for a while the precipitate will become crystalline. It may be necessary to rub inside of beaker with a glass stirring rod to bring about crystallization.

Procaine hydrochloride (method 2): Dissolve 100 mg of the material in 5 ml of water. Add 2 drops of dilute sulfuric acid and stir. Add 5 drops of 0.1 N potassium permanganate test solution. If the material is procaine hydrochloride, the purple-brown tint of the permanganate will disappear.

Lidocaine hydrochloride: To 10 ml of a 2.5% solution of the material, add sodium hydroxide solution until pH indication is alkaline. Filter this solution. Wash the residue in the filter with water several times.

Dissolve 100 mg of the residue in 1 ml of alcohol. Add 0.5 ml (10 drops) of a 10% cobalt chloride solution to this. Shake well for 2 minutes. If the material is lidocaine hydrochloride, a fine, bluish-green precipitate will form.

Lidocaine (free base): If this is the suspected identity of the material, do not treat with sodium hydroxide and filter. Simply dissolve 100 mg of the material in 1 ml of alcohol, add 10 drops of cobalt chloride solution and shake. If the material is free-base lidocaine, a fine, bluish-green precipitate will form.

Lactose: To 5 ml of a 1:20 solution of the material, add 5 ml of 5% sodium hydroxide solution. Warm the mixture gently. If the material is lactose, the solution will first become yellow, then turn to reddish-brown.

Sucrose: To 100 mg of the material add 2 ml of dilute sulfuric acid. Boil. Add 4 ml of 5% sodium hydroxide solution and 3 ml of Fehling's test solution. Heat to boiling. If the material is sucrose, a red to dark red precipitate will form.

Lactose-Sucrose difference verification (method 1): Dissolve 50 mg of the material in 5 ml of water. Add 1 ml of copper (II) acetate solution and heat the light blue liquid for 10 minutes on a water bath. No more than a greenish tint should occur if the material is lactose. If a finely-dispersed red precipitate occurs, the material is sucrose. Add 2 ml of sodium hydroxide to the liquid, and heat for another 2 minutes. If the material is lactose, a voluminous brick-red precipitate occurs. This will not occur of the material is sucrose.

Lactose-Sucrose difference verification (method 2): To 500 mg of the material add 1 ml of concentrated nitric acid. Heat the mixture for 30 minutes in a water bath. Allow the mixture to cool to room temperature. Dilute with 1 ml of water. Allow the mixture to stand for 1 hour at room temperature, but shake every 10 minutes. If the material is lactose, a voluminous white precipitate will slowly form. This will not occur if the material is sucrose.

Inositol (method 1): To 1 ml of a 1:50 solution of the material, add 6 ml nitric acid. Evaporate to dryness on a water bath. Dissolve the residue in 0.5 ml of a 1:10 solution of strontium nitrate. Evaporate the residue to dryness as before. If the material is inositol, the residue will have a red-purple color.

Inositol (method 2): To 4 ml of a 1:100 solution of the material, add 1 ml of lead subacetate test solution. Heat in a water bath for 5 minutes. If the material is inositol, the solution will become a translucent gel.

Mannitol: To 1 ml of a saturated solution of the material, add 0.5 ml of ferric chloride test solution. Then add 0.25 ml of sodium hyroxide solution. Shake well. A clear solution is obtained. It remains clear upon further addition of sodium hydroxide solution.

Corn Starch: Add several drops of tincture of iodine to a small amount of a solution of the suspected material and shake. If corn starch is present, the mixture will turn a deep blue or purplish-blue. Upon heating, the color will disappear. Upon cooling, the color will reappear.

Methionine (method 1): Saturate 1 ml of sulfuric acid with anhydrous cupric sulfate. Add this to 25 mg of the material. If the material is methionine a yellow color appears.

Methionine (method 2): Dissolve 5 mg of the material in 5 ml of water. Add 2 ml of sodium hydroxide test solution. Add 0.3 ml of sodium nitroprusside test solution while shaking vigorously. When the latter has been added, shake well again. Allow it to stand at 35–40°C for 10 minutes. Cool it in an ice bath for 2 minutes. Add 2 ml of dilute hydrochloric acid. Shake well. If the material is methionine, the solution will turn red.

Talc: Thoroughly mix 200 mg of the material with 900 mg of anhydrous sodium carbonate. Heat the mixture in a platinum or nickel crucible until fusion is complete. After cooling, combine the fused mixture with 50 ml of hot water in a beaker. Add hydrochloric acid by drops. Effervescence will occur. Continue adding acid until effervescence ceases. Then add another 10 ml of the acid. Evaporate the mixture to dryness on a water bath. Upon cooling add 20 ml of water. Boil and filter. Add 10 ml of a 1:10000 solution of methylene blue to the residue. Wash with water. If material was talc, a blue precipitate will appear. To further verify, dissolve 2 g of ammonium chloride and 5 ml of ammonia test solution in the filtrate obtained in the preceding steps. Filter solution if necessary. Add disodium hydrogen phosphate test solution by drops while stirring. If the original material was talc, a white precipitate will form.

Talc sprinkled on the surface of water will accumulate there in lumps without sedimenting.

Epsom salts: This requires separate tests for magnesium and for sulfate. *Magnesium:* Dissolve 50 mg of the material in 1 ml of water and add 1 ml of ammonia solution. A white precipitate forms which dissolves in an excess of ammonium chloride solution. *Sulfate:* Acidify the above solution with 2 ml of hydrochloric acid and add 1 ml of barium chloride solution. A white precipitate occurs.

Boric acid (method 1): Dissolve 50 mg of the material in 5 ml of water and add 1 drop of hydrochloric acid. Moisten a strip of turmeric paper with this solution and dry. The paper turns pink and changes to blue or greenish-black upon addition of 1 drop of sodium hydroxide solution.

Boric acid (method 2): Dissolve 100 mg of the material in 5 ml of alcohol in a porcelain dish. When ignited, it burns with a green-bordered flame.

Methedrine (method 1): Combine 2 drops of formaldehyde with 3 ml sulfuric acid. Add 3 drops of this to 1 mg of the material. If the material is methedrine, the mixture will turn brick-red immediately, then soon become brown and slowly change to dull olive-green.

Methedrine (method 2): To 5 ml of a 1:100 solution of the material, add 0.5 ml of mercuric chloride test solution. If the material is methedrine, a white crystalline precipitate will form.

Methedrine (method 3): To 5 ml of a 1:100 solution of the material, add 0.5 ml of iodine test solution. If the material is methedrine, a brown precipitate will form.

Methedrine (method 4): To 5 ml of a 1:100 solution of the material, add 0.5 ml of picric acid test solution. If the material is methedrine, a yellow crystalline precipitate will form.

Caffeine (method 1): To 10 mg of the material in a porcelain dish, add 1 drop of concentrated hydrogen peroxide solution and 5 drops of 25% hydrochloric acid. Evaporate to dryness. The orange-red residue dissolves in a few drops of ammonia solution and turns crimson.

Caffeine (method 2): To 10 mg of the material in a porcelain dish, add 1 ml of hydrochloric acid and 100 mg of potassium chlorate. Evaporate to dryness. Expose residue to vapors of dilute ammonia solution. A purple color appears, which disappears upon addition of a fixed alkali solution.

Caffeine (method 3): To a saturated solution of the material add tannic acid solution. A white precipitate occurs which dissolves in an excess of the reagent.

Ephedrine (method 1): Dissolve 50 mg of the material in 1 ml of water. Add 3 drops of copper (II) sulfate solution. Add 1 ml of sodium hydroxide solution. A violet color appears. To the mixture add an equal volume of butanol, and shake. The butanol layer turns reddish-violet.

Ephedrine (method 2): Dissolve 50 mg of the material in 5 ml of water. Add a few drops of sodium hydroxide solution. Add 2 ml of potassium hexacyanferrate (III) solution and heat. The odor of benzaldehyde evolves.

Quinine sulfate (method 1): Dissolve 10 mg of the material in 10 ml of water. Add 2 or 3 drops of dilute sulfuric acid. If the material is quinine sulfate, a blue fluorescence is produced.

Quinine sulfate (method 2): To 5 ml of a 1:1000 solution of the material, add 1 or 2 drops of standard bromine test solution and 1 ml of standard ammonia test solution. If the material is quinine sulfate, the mixture will soon turn green.

Yohimbine hydrochloride (method 1): Dissolve 10 mg of the material in 1 ml of concentrated sulfuric acid, then add a small crystal of potassium dichromate. Violet streaks will appear. The solution will turn slate-blue and then green.

Yohimbine hydrochloride (method 2): Add 3 drops of fuming nitric acid to 10 mg of the material. A dark green color appears, changing to yellow. Upon addition of 2 ml of 10% ethanolic potassium hydroxide solution, the color changes to cherry-red.

Pemoline (microscopic crystal tests): Treated with picric acid, produces blades and serrated plates (sensitivity: 1 in 1000). Treated with trinitrobenzoic acid solution, produces long plates best viewed under polarized light (sensitivity: 1 in 1000).

Phencyclidine (microscopic crystal tests): Treated with gold bromide solution, produces small oily crystals best viewed under polarized light (sensitivity: 1 in

1000). Treated with potassium permanganate solution, produces small irregular plates (sensitivity: 1 in 1000).

There are several tests for identifying a sample as cocaine.

Permanganate Test: To 5 ml of a 2% solution of cocaine hydrochloride, add 3 drops of dilute sulfuric acid and stir. Add one drop of a 1% solution of potassium permanganate. If there was a full 2% of cocaine hydrochloride in the original solution, it should take on a pink tint after the permanganate solution is added, and that should not entirely disappear during the next 30 minutes. When added to a stronger cocaine solution, there should be a precipitation of rhombic plates which decompose upon heating. If cinnamyl-cocaine is presnt, there will be an odor of bitter almonds during decomposition.

Maclagan Test: When a few drops of ammonia solution are added to a saturated solution of any salt of cocaine and vigorously stirred with a glass rod, any amorphous alkaloids present will be converted into their free bases and will separate out as oily drops and form a milky solution. If the cocaine is pure, there will be a deposit of crystals on the rod and the sides of the beaker within 5 minutes. If isoatropyl-cocaine is present, there will be no crystallization and the solution will turn milky. This test is not suitable for determining the purity of street cocaine, but is used to tell if the sample is of pure pharmaceutical quality or if it still contains the various companion alkaloids of the coca leaf.

Odor Test #1: This test shows if cocaine is present at all. The sample in its solid state is treated with fuming nitric acid (sp. gr. 1.4), evaporated to dryness, and treated once more with a strong solution of potassium hydroxide in methanol. This is stirred with a glass rod. If cocaine is present, stirring will produce an odor reminiscent of oil of peppermint.

Odor Test #2: Add 100 mg of the material to 1 ml of sulfuric acid. Heat the mixture on a water bath to 100°C for 5 minutes. Cautiously add this to 2 ml of water. If the material is cocaine hydrochloride, there will be an aromatic odor of methyl benzoate. When the solution is cooled and allowed to stand for several hours, crystals of benzoic acid will separate.

Chromium Test: Dissolve 100 mg of the material in 5 ml of water. Add 5 drops of a 1:20 solution of chromium trioxide. If the material is cocaine hydrochloride, a yellow precipitate will form. When the mixture is heated on a water bath and stirred, the precipitate redissolves. When 1 ml of hydrochloric acid is added, an orange-yellow precipitate is formed.

PURIFICATION OF COCAINE

Improvement of Quality

REMOVAL OF CUTS

Because cocaine hydrochloride and many of the substances used to cut it have different solubilities, these cuts can be easily separated from the product. One of the most obvious examples of this is cocaine cut with talc. Talc is insoluble in almost any standard solvent, including water. To remove the talc from the cocaine, one need only dissolve the product thoroughly in hot distilled water, pass it through a filter paper, pass some more hot water through the filter to rinse through any remaining cocaine, and evaporate the collected liquids on a hot oil bath. The insoluble talc remains behind in the filter while the soluble cocaine hydrochloride passes through with the water and is completely recovered after evaporation. The purpose of the oil bath is to maintain a temperature slightly above the boiling point of water so that the cocaine will not be decomposed. Other cocaine hydrochloride solvents, such as alcohol or chloroform, can be used instead of water. They have the advantage of evaporating at lower temperatures than water and can be evaporated on a water bath instead of an oil bath. Precautions must be taken, however, to remove their toxic fumes, and, in the case of alcohol, to avoid combustion. Details of the correct procedures are given later in this chapter.

Talc, unlike the other adulterants, is almost universally insoluble and is therefore most easy to remove. Many of the other cuts, however, are insoluble in some solvents which do dissolve cocaine hydrochloride. By referring to the Solvent Chart below one may find, for a given cut, a solvent which can be used for this purpose. For example: assume that the cocaine has been adulterated with lactose. Upon examination of the chart we find that cocaine hydrochloride is soluble in either water, alcohol or chloroform. Lactose, we find, is insoluble in ether or chloroform, and only slightly soluble in cool alcohol. Ether, although not a solvent for lactose, is useless in this case because cocaine hydrochloride is also insoluble in it. Chloroform, on the other hand, is a fairly good solvent for cocaine, but it will not dissolve lactose.

To separate the lactose from the cocaine, one need only dissolve the product in chloroform and carry out the same basic procedure described above for removing talc. Chloroform is used for washing the residue in the filter, and the collected liquids are then evaporated on a water bath. The product will be free of lactose and any other cut that is insoluble in chloroform, such as inositol and, to some extent, quinine sulfate.

If chloroform is not available, referring once more to the chart we find that lactose is only very slightly soluble in cool alcohol. If cool alcohol is used in place

Substance	Soluble	Very slightly soluble	Insoluble
Cocaine hydrochloride	Water Alcohol Chloroform Acetone		Ether Benzene
Procaine hydrochloride	Alcohol Water	Chloroform	Ether
Procaine (free base)	Alcohol Ether Chloroform Benzene	Water	
Tetracaine hydrochloride	Water Alcohol		Ether Benzene
Benzocaine	Ether Alcohol Chloroform Water (acidic)	Water (non-acidic)	

Substance	Soluble	Very slightly soluble	Insoluble
Butacaine sulfate	Water Warm alcohol Acetone	Chloroform	Ether
Lidocaine hydrochloride	Water Alcohol Chloroform		Ether Benzene Petroleum ether
Lidocaine (free base)	Ether Alcohol Chloroform Benzene		Cold water
Methedrine	Alcohol Water Chloroform		Ether
Pemoline	Alcohol Organic solvents		Ether Cold water

Substance	Soluble	Very slightly soluble	Insoluble
Yohimbine hydrochloride	Hot water	Cold water Cold alcohol	Ether Acetone
Ephedrine sulfate	Water	Ether	Chloroform
Caffeine	Ether Hot acetone	Isopropanol Cold acetone	
Quinine sulfate	Hot ethanol	Hot water Chloroform	Ether Cold water
Lactose Dextrose Sucrose	Water	Cold alcohol	Ether Chloroform Acetone

Substance	Soluble	Very slightly soluble	Insoluble
Mannitol	Water Pyridine Aniline	Alcohol	Ether
Inositol	Water		Chloroform Ether Alcohol (absolute)
Epsom salts	Water		Alcohol (absolute)
Talc			All standard solvents Water Alcohol Chloroform etc.

of chloroform, not all, but most, of the lactose will be removed. This should be sufficient for most purposes. Both quinine sulfate and procaine hydrochloride are only very slightly soluble in chloroform. If coke that contains either or both of these cuts is treated in the above manner with this solvent, most of the adulterant will remain in the filter, while the cocaine/chloroform solution passes through. This partial removal is inadequate for precise estimation of the percentage of the cut, as described under Solvent Test in the previous chapter. Still, it will greatly improve the purity of the cocaine. This is especially important in the case of quinine adulteration (see toxic effects of quinine sulfate in the chapter on adulterants).

If the cocaine has been cut with benzocaine, or free-base lidocaine, reference once more to the chart discloses that these substances are soluble in ether, whereas cocaine hydrochloride is not. Because of this, a reverse of the preceding solvent filtration technique may be employed. Under these circumstances the product is dissolved in ether, passed through the filter, and washed with more ether. The ether passes through the filter, carrying with it the soluble cuts. These liquids can be discarded. The cocaine hydrochloride is then retrieved from the filter and dried. Any cocaine that cannot be removed manually, including that which has impregnated the filter paper, can then be washed through with chloroform or any cocaine hydrochloride solvent and the solvent evaporated to yield the salvaged cocaine.

Reconstitution of cocaine by evaporation should be conducted in a dry atmosphere. If it is humid, the product is likely to take up moisture and assume a

gummy texture. This often happens when the evaporation has just been completed, but the product usually becomes normal after standing a few hours. In
some cases it may be necessary to dry it further in a
desiccator for 24 hours. There may be instances in
which the gummy product cannot be made normal by
desiccation. In the past, we were not certain what
caused this. Recently, a group of our associates in
Seattle analyzed a sample of cocaine that behaved in
this manner and found that it contained the coca alkaloid ecgonine. They also found that the problem
could be rectified by treating the product with 28-
percent ammonium hydroxide solution to convert the
hydrochlorides to their free-base forms, drying and
desiccating this, redissolving it in ethyl ether, carefully titrating this with hydrochloric acid to return the
alkaloids to their hydrochloride forms, evaporating to
dryness, and desiccating. The Seattle group also discovered that a heavy (40 percent or more) lidocaine
hydrochloride cut could have the same gumming effect
on cocaine.

All of this information was received only a few days
before these additions to the new edition of *Pleasures
of Cocaine* were written. At this time, we have not as
yet had the opportunity to verify the Seattle group's
findings. If the chemically inclined reader wishes to
experiment with this procedure, it is suggested that he
work, at first, with small samples until he is certain
that he can carry it off successfully. When doing any
solvent-removal of cuts, it is best to test a small sample
first to see if it is likely to remain gummy.

Although cocaine that has this gummy texture is
impossible to snort, it is still cocaine and active. It can

be smoked on foil (The Coke Smoke), added to a
liqueur (see Cocaine Cordial), or dissolved in water
(see Liquid Lady).

PREPARATIONS OF DIFFERENT
FORMS OF COCAINE

Cocaine hydrochloride may appear in any one of three
basic forms: rocks, flakes, or fine powder. The latter
form is simply the result of rock or flake cocaine
becoming crushed either intentionally or through
packaging, handling or transportation. Any of these
forms can be easily converted into any other form.
There is no difference in potency between one form
and another. These methods of conversion are mentioned here only because many dealers and consumers
have attached folkloric value to certain forms of
cocaine. It is worth remembering that, no matter what
form of coke you have, it must be reduced to powder
before snorting.

Flake Cocaine

There are two types of flake cocaine: precipitated and
reconstituted. The first is the product of the conversion of free-base cocaine to its hydrochloride while it
is in a solvent in which the free base is soluble but the
salt is not. The second is made from cocaine hydrochloride which has been dissolved in a solvent (methanol) and reconstituted to a solid by evaporating it in
droplets on a hot, flat surface.

Precipitated Flake Cocaine

To prepare this product it is necessary to start with free-base cocaine. This can be prepared from any salt of cocaine by treating it with ammonium hydroxide solution and evaporating off the water in a hot oil bath. Flakes of cocaine hydrochloride can be obtained by dissolving the free base in 5 parts of ether and adding hydrochloric acid by drops (titration). Flakes of cocaine hydrochloride will precipitate like snow-flakes. When further addition of hydrochloric acid produces no more precipitate, the ether and flakes are filtered. The ether will pass through the filter along with any unreacted free-base cocaine. The cocaine hydrochloride will remain in the filter and can be washed with another portion of ether, collected and dried.

All of the ether which has passed through the filter can be treated once more with hydrochloric acid to convert any unreacted free-base cocaine remaining from the previous titration. This solution is then filtered, the filtrant is washed with ether as before, and the cocaine hydrochloride is collected and dried. To salvage any cocaine hydrochloride lingering in the filter paper, methanol is passed through the filter, collected and evaporated.

The cocaine hydrochloride precipitated from the ether will be flakes of even size. If the coke has been cut with any ether-soluble adulterant, this will pass through the filter and be separated from the product. If the coke contains any methanol-soluble (but ether-insoluble) cuts, these will remain in the coke and pass through the filter with the residual cocaine hydrochloride when washed with methanol. The cocaine flakes retrieved from the methanol washing, unlike the precipitated flakes, will not be of even size.

Except for the fact that some of the cuts may be removed during the process, there is little value in converting cocaine hydrochloride to the free base and reconverting it to precipitated flakes. Furthermore, wherever titration and filtration are involved, a small percentage of loss of the product is inevitable. 1000 grams of cocaine hydrochloride converted to free base, precipitated as a salt and filtered may yield only 998 or 999 grams of the final product.

Reconstituted Flake

This method is much simpler than preparing precipitated flake and entails no loss of material. The different types of reconstituted flakes produced by the methods below are sometimes referred to as "counterfeit flakes," although there is nothing counterfeit about the quality of the cocaine produced in these manners. These flakes, unlike the precipitated product, are not of even size.

Thin Flakes

To produce these, dissolve cocaine hydrochloride in methanol, using 50 ml of solvent for each gram of cocaine. Place a Pyrex casserole in a water bath and deposit drops of the solution—one drop at a time—on different portions of the bottom of the casserole. The methanol will evaporate almost immediately, leaving a thin, flaky crust on the glass. When the entire bottom has been covered, this is scraped up with a single-edge razor blade and collected. The process is repeated until all of the solution has been evaporated and all of the flakes collected.

Thick Opalescent Flakes

These are sometimes called "mother of pearl" cocaine. They are made in much the same way as the above except that 1) a more concentrated solution (20 ml of methanol per gram of cocaine) is used, and 2) after the bottom of the casserole has been covered and the methanol evaporated, another layer of drops is deposited upon the previous layer. This crust can be built up as thickly as desired by depositing more layers on top of each other. Always wait for the preceding layer to dry before more drops are deposited. When the composite of layers is thick enough, it is scraped up and collected.

Thin Transparent Flakes

These are flakes produced essentially in the same manner as the thin flakes described above, except that prior to evaporation, activated charcoal (Norite) is added to the methanol/cocaine solution. The mixture is shaken well for several minutes and then filtered. The Norite, which will remain in the filter, is washed with several portions of methanol, and the collected filtrates are evaporated by drops in the same manner described above under Thin Flakes. The Norite removes colored impurities from the cocaine, rendering the final product more transparent. Many dealers and consumers are greatly impressed by this form of cocaine. This process does something for the appear-

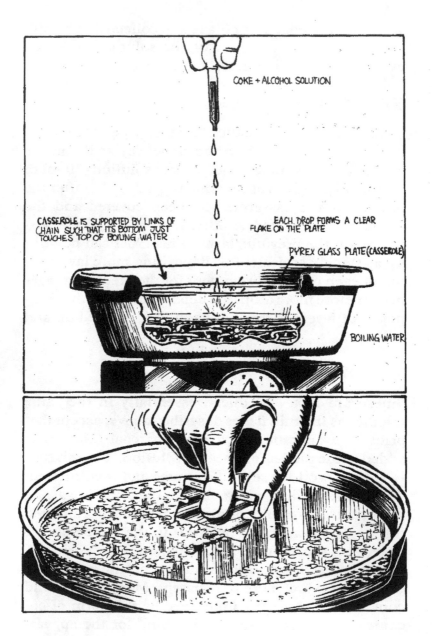

ance of cocaine but does nothing to improve its actual quality or effectiveness. Because filtration is involved, there may be some loss of yield.

When flakes of cocaine have been reconstituted from methanol solution, minute amounts of the solvent may linger in the product. For this reason it is advisable to spread the collected cocaine no more than ¼ inch deep on a flat tray in a warm, dry place exposed to the air, but protected from dust, and allow it to sit for 24 hours before using it. Methanol (wood alcohol) is a toxic substance. If the above instructions are followed correctly, it is safe to use as a solvent because none will remain in the product.

Rock Cocaine

The attractiveness of this form of cocaine has been discussed elsewhere in this book. It has been mentioned that many dealers and consumers erroneously believe that if cocaine is in rock form it must be free of adulterants. Cocaine can be reconstituted along with its adulterants into fine-looking rocks. Many unscrupulous dealers will combine a cut with flake or powdered cocaine and reconstitute it into rocks to impress their customers with its "purity."

To make rock cocaine, prepare a solution of 5 ml of methanol for each gram of cocaine. Fill the casserole to ¼ of its height with this solution and evaporate it on the water bath until all of the methanol has been removed. The temperature of the water bath should be just hot enough that the methanol solution boils slowly. Do not let it boil over. It is best that the water not be boiling when the methanol solution is added to the casserole. The water temperature can then be raised as needed to effect evaporation. When the methanol is gone and a dry layer of cocaine about ¼ inch thick remains at the bottom of the casserole, this solid is chipped away with a knife or ice pick and collected. Because of its greater thickness, rock cocaine prepared in this manner is even more likely to contain residual methanol than is flake cocaine. It should be spread in a tray and allowed to "dry out" as described above, but for at least 48 hours.

DATA ON CONDUCTING
LABORATORY PROCEDURES

In the preceding chapters mention has been made of various elementary laboratory procedures such as filtration, oil or water baths, and evaporation. Since many readers may not know how to conduct these procedures correctly and safely, detailed explanations of them are given here. Several of the solvents called for in the purification and improvement of cocaine are dangerous if handled improperly. Instructions are given for working safely with these materials.

Hot Bath

This is a double-boiler system in which a beaker or other open glass or stainless container is heated in a pan of another liquid. The purpose of the bath is to heat the contents of the beaker to a given temperature above which it cannot possibly go. For example, when the content of the beaker is ethanol (boiling point 78.5°C) or chloroform (b.p. 61.2°C), water (b.p. 100°C) is employed in the bath. This prevents the solvent in the beaker from going above that temperature. These measures help to avoid accidental fire from flammable solvent fumes and prevent scorching of the material dissolved in the solvent during the last stages of evaporation. If water is the solvent, oil, which has a much higher boiling point, is used in the bath. A hot-plate electric—rather than gas—range is used as the heat source for a hot bath. The beaker should not be placed directly above the heating element unless a separator is placed between the bath pan and the beaker.

When evaporating any solvent other than water, adequate ventilation must be arranged to remove the fumes. Many solvents are highly combustible and their fumes are explosive if permitted to accumulate in a closed area. Some solvents, such as methanol, are very toxic if inhaled. Even ethanol (grain alcohol), the least toxic of the common solvents, may cause intoxication if its fumes are inhaled to excess. A fume-hood should be employed to carry off solvent vapors. This is an inverted funnel-shaped structure suspended above the evaporation beaker, leading by way of a flue system to an exhaust fan with a spark-free motor.

Ether is the most flammably dangerous of the solvents. It demands extremely cautious handling. It evaporates rapidly at room temperature (b.p. 34.5°C). Prolonged breathing of its fumes can cause unconsciousness, but the greatest danger is that the smallest spark can ignite them. When ether is being used there must be no source of ignition in the room. This includes flame, lighted cigarette, spark or glowing heat-

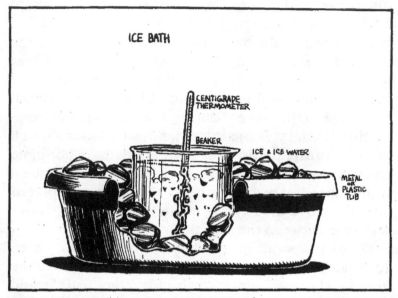

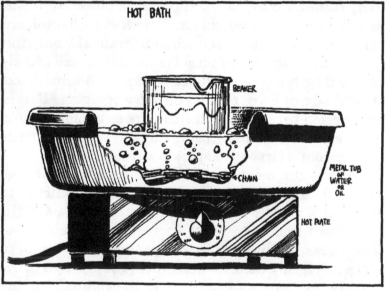

ing element. Any fan motors used must be spark-free. Doorbells and telephones must be disconnected so that no spark occurs. All furnace and boiler flames—including the pilot lights—must be extinguished. All electrical plugs that might arc in wall sockets must be disconnected. Loose fluorescent lamps may provide a spark and should be turned off or have their points of connection shielded with electrical tape. It is best to work by daylight and to have no electricity functioning in the room except for the spark-free exhaust fan.

Another danger with ether is that it draws oxygen from the atmosphere and forms peroxides. If ether contains peroxides, it will explode upon distillation. Never distill ether without first testing for the presence of peroxides. Peroxides can be removed from ether by treating it with ferrous sulfate solution, that has been made slightly acidic with sodium bisulfate, until peroxide test reads negative.

Ether must be stored sealed in a cool place. Never store ether unsealed in a frost-free refrigerator. The vacuum may draw the vapors into the motor and ignite them.

When working with ether, it should be chilled to minimize evaporation. Open containers of ether should be kept in an ice bath during all operations except evaporation. High temperatures are not used to evaporate ether. It is usually evaporated at room temperature or in a preheated warm water bath using a sparkless vacuum pump. After the fumes reach the pump, they must be led directly to a safe place outdoors where they can disperse.

Desiccation

Traces of a solvent and water remaining in the product after evaporation can be removed either by placing it for 30 minutes in an oven preheated to 300°F and then turned off, or by placing it overnight in a desiccator. This is an inverted bell jar over a shelf, on top of which is the product and beneath which is some hygroscopic (moisture-absorbing) material such as magnesium sulfate, sodium sulfate, calcium chloride or sulfuric acid.

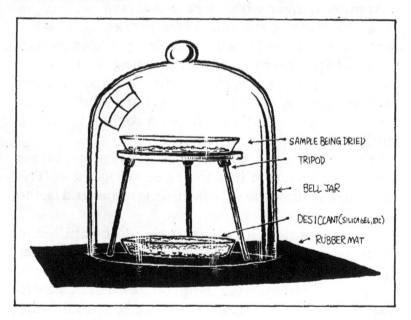

SAMPLE BEING DRIED

TRIPOD

BELL JAR

DESICCANT (SILICA GEL, ETC)

RUBBER MAT

Filtration

When a mixture of solid substances is shaken in a solvent and poured through a filter, those substances that are soluble in that solvent will pass through the

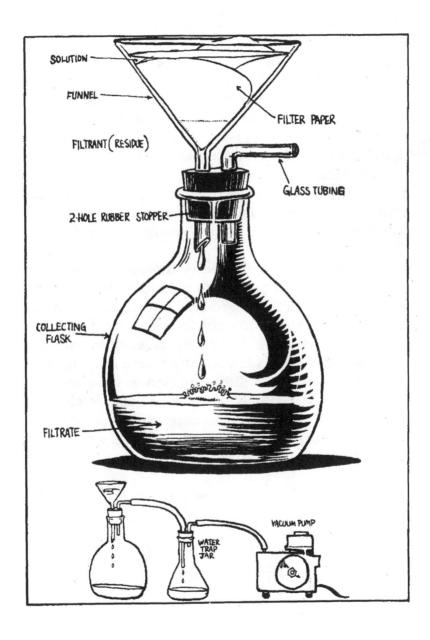

filter in solution, while those that are not soluble in it will remain behind as residue. This method of separation is quite useful in removing adulterants from cocaine. A simple filtering apparatus consists of a paper filter (various meshes available) in the cup of a Buchner funnel inserted in a collection flask. A somewhat more efficient system involves the use of suction. To do so, all glassware must be fitted tightly with two-hole rubber stoppers, and a trap jar should be fitted between the collection flask and the vacuum source. The pump must be strong enough to draw the solution through, but gentle enough not to rupture the paper.

The material which passes through the filter is called the filtrate. That which remains in the filter cup is called the filtrant or residue. To wash the filtrant or the filter paper means to pour the solvent into the filter and let it pass through by drip or suction into the collection flask. This is done to retrieve or remove all residual traces of the soluble substance. In some cases the filtrant material may be thick and tend to clog the filter paper. This is likely to happen when separating talc from cocaine. To prevent clogging, a filter cell (Celite) can be placed in the filter beforehand.

CULTIVATION OF COCA

ENVIRONMENT

Coca is native to the Andes of Peru and Bolivia. It does best on moist warm slopes from 1500 to 5000 feet elevation in Peru and as high as 6000 feet in Bolivia. Here the temperature ranges between 64°F and 86°F, usually remaining between 64°F and 68°F. Coca may grow well at somewhat higher temperatures than 86°F, but will yield less alkaloids. Frost or long continued cold will kill the plant even during its dormant stage. Coca flourishes in the regions where coffee, maize, cacao, sugar cane, banana and other fruit are also grown. The coca shrub requires an environment where the atmosphere is humid and there is some drizzle or mist nearly every day. If coca is grown in an area where there is heavy rain lasting a month or more, the plant will produce profuse foliage, but its alkaloid yield will be low.

There is some debate as to how much the elevation influences alkaloid yield. In Java, experiments showed no significant difference in yield from plants grown at different elevations. Coca growers of Peru, however, claim that higher altitudes bring higher concentration of alkaloids, the limit on this being elevations at

which there is probability of frost. It is possible that
the greater mineral content in the Peruvian soil at
higher levels increases the yield. This is true of other
plants. The San Pedro cactus, which is native to these
regions, produces a greater concentration of mesca-
line in the mineral-rich soil of these altitudes. The
aromatic principles of the coffee bean are improved in
these mountainous regions. It has also been suggested that the slower growth at higher elevations
allows for greater accumulation of alkaloids. The
leaves of coca grown at 5000 to 6000 feet are much
smaller and less profuse than those produced at 2000
feet, but the leaf quality and content are greater. Also,
such plants give forth enough foliage for but one
harvest annually. Another explanation of the greater
alkaloidal production at high altitudes is that the
atmospheric electricity at these levels somewhat increases nitrogen fixation in the soil.

SOIL

Coca flourishes best in soils rich in humus and well
fixed with nitrogen. The soil should be rich in mineral matter but free from limestone. If there is limestone present, even in the substratum, it will stunt the
plant's growth and very scant foliage will be produced.
Most Andean soil contains iron disulfide schists with
organic matter and mineral salts from decaying vege-
tation. The very best quality leaf is grown at Phara in
Peru, where the adjacent mountains are rich in arse-
nical pyrites. These factors may have much influence
on alkaloidal production.

Usually, coca grown in the greenhouse has an extremely low yield of alkaloids. Extensive experimentation, however, has shown that coca grown under such conditions succeeds best when a mixture of sand and leafmold is used.

Good drainage is essential or the delicate roots of the plant will rot. This drainage is naturally provided by the slopes of the Andes, where it is normally grown. In these regions it has been found that young coca plants do best in light, porous soil, while full-grown shrubs yield better-quality leaf in soil that tends to have a more clayish character. If the clay content of the soil is high, this will place some limitation on the drainage. In this case the slope of the land is important to provide the necessary drainage.

PROPAGATION

Coca can be grown either from the seed or from cuttings. The latter is the method most frequently used. This is so for several reasons. The seed has a very short duration of viability and cannot be stored longer than for a few weeks. Different varieties as well as different individual plants have different qualities, both in foliage and alkaloidal yield, so there is much to be gained by propagating from the very best plants rather than taking chances on seeds whose source of pollination is most likely unknown. Because plants grown from the seed must go through development from the seedling stage, it takes them longer than cuttings to yield mature leaf.

PROPAGATION FROM THE SEED

This involves collecting the seeds, preparing them for planting, caring for them and transplanting them to their final growing site.

PREPARATION OF THE SEED

The fruit of the coca shrub looks much like a cranberry. It is gathered when scarlet during the march harvest season. This must be done before the fruit begins to turn dark brown or black and shrivel. Decayed fruit is discarded. The rest are put in water. Those that float have been attacked by insects and are discarded. The ones that sink are collected and put in

a damp, shaded place for a few days. This allows the flesh of the fruit to rot just enough that the seed can be easily removed. These seeds should be washed and then dried in the sun for a few hours. They should be planted immediately. If they are to be preserved longer, they must be dried in the sun immediately after they are gathered from the plant. After several days of drying, the fleshy part of the fruit is reduced to a protective coating. Under the best circumstances in Peru, seeds dried in this manner may retain their viability for as much as two weeks. In the greenhouse it is usually difficult to preserve the seed and get it to germinate. Here the general practice is to plant the seed fresh without drying.

STARTING THE SEED

The seeds are started in a nursery during the rainy season before spring. Some growers like to sprout them first. To do this the seeds are heaped in piles 3-4 inches high and watered several times a day until they germinate. Then they are carefully picked apart and sown in the nursery on well-turned soil. A mixture of 3 parts humus, 2 parts fairly coarse sand and 1 part leaf mold is excellent for raising the seedlings. This mixture should be kept wet for two weeks before sowing and should be damp when the seeds are planted. After the seeds are on the soil they are covered with a thin layer of sand, just enough to cover them. Don't give them too much water, but don't let the surface of the soil get dry. Sprinkle it frequently but lightly if it tends to dry out, or mist it down several times a day with an atomizer. Birds love to eat coca seeds. If the nursery is outdoors, a cloth cover should be placed over the seed bed until the plants have germinated. The first shoots should appear in about two weeks. They must be protected from getting too much sun.

CULTIVATION OF YOUNG PLANTS

As the seedlings begin to establish themselves as plants and are about 6 inches tall, they should be thinned out to about 12 inches apart. The soil beneath them should be at least a foot in depth. Never let the soil dry out at more than an inch below the surface. The temperature should remain between 64°F and 86°F. If the atmosphere is dry, spray the foliage with a plant mister once or twice a day. Keep out weeds. The plants must be cared for in the nursery for 6–12 months from germination before they can be transplanted.

TRANSPLANTING

When the plants are 16–20 inches high they should be transplanted to their final growing site. This can be either a flat field of well-tilled, humus-rich soil with good drainage, or a slope of rich soil with a fairly high content of red clay, where the inclination of the land affords sufficient drainage to compensate for the less porous clay soil. The site should be well watered two days before transplanting; so should the nursery plants.

The root system of the coca plant is like a massive

wig. Dig carefully 6 inches away from the base of the plant, leaving as much soil about the roots as possible. Probe as deeply as possible so as not to sever the taproots.

Holes should be dug 4–6 feet apart in the new location, large enough to accommodate the soil-covered roots of the plants. After these are placed in the ground, any remaining spaces about the roots should be filled with porous soil similar to that in which the young plants were raised. The base of the plant is then watered. The soil may sink a little after watering. More soil is then added to the hollow, so that there is a small mound about the plant.

Transplanting should be done in the late afternoon, so that the plants have some time to adapt to their new location before the hot sun threatens them. If the weather is likely to be misty or foggy for one or more days after transplanting, so much the better. If the sun seems to be making the transplants wilt, they should be covered with paper bags for a few days and then gradually introduced to sunlight by giving them a few hours of exposure the first day in the early morning and late afternoon and increasing exposure by one more hour each subsequent day until they are receiving a full day of light. It is also helpful to spray the foliage of the transplants with water several times a day, especially if the weather is hot and dry. In some districts of the Andes coca plants are intercropped with squash, corn, or coffee to shade the young plants.

PROPAGATION FROM CUTTINGS

This method of propagation is much less involved
than growing from the seed. A slip 8–12 inches long
is cut from a mature plant just above the axis. The
base of the cutting can be dipped in a rooting agent

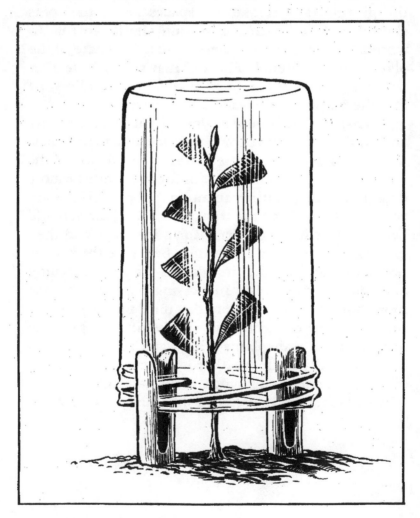

such as Rootone to encourage root growth and prevent fungal decay. The cutting is then inserted 3–4
inches deep in damp sand. If the slip has a lot of
foliage on it, this should be reduced because there will
not be enough roots for some time to support this
much foliage. One of the best ways to do this is to cut
each leaf in half. Cover the cutting with a jar for two
weeks or so to retain the plant's moisture, but leave an
inch of air space between the jar and the ground so the
plant can breathe. Leave the cutting in the sand and
keep it damp. After a month or so the plant will begin
to produce more abundant foliage. This is an indication that the roots are developing well. Let them gain
strength for 3–4 more weeks before transplanting.
When transplanting, treat these plants the same as
when transplanting seed-grown plants.

HARVESTING

After 18–24 months the leaves will take on a faint
yellow tint, lose their original softness and become
more brittle. They are now mature and ripe for picking. This is about eight days before they would fall
anyway. The leafstem is pinched and each leaf carefully stripped so as not to injure the tender twigs. Only
the mature leaves are removed. Picking these leaves
encourages growth of more foliage.

There are usually three annual harvests in the
Andes, except at extremely high altitudes, where there
is only one per year. The first harvest is in March.
There is a smaller harvest at the end of June and
another regular harvest around October or November.

The coca plant in its natural setting grows about 12 feet high. For convenience of harvesting the shrubs are usually kept pruned to around 3–6 feet by picking off the upper twigs at harvest time. This is also beneficial to the plant and encourages lateral growth.

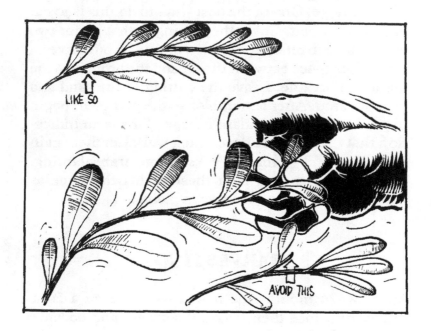

DRYING AND CURING OF LEAVES

Harvesting should always be done during dry weather. If the leaves get wet before harvesting, they are likely to rot and lose their alkaloidal content. Morning is the proper time for collecting the leaves so that advantage can be taken of the hot sun of late morning and early afternoon. Drying preserves the alkaloids. The sooner it is done, the more alkaloids are retained.

The freshly-gathered leaves are spread an inch or two thick on dry slabs in the hot sun. If the sun is hot enough so that they can dry in 6 hours, the leaf will be of the highest quality. Such fast-dried leaves are known in Peru as *coca del día* and command the greatest price. The leaves should be slighlty crisp but not dried to brittleness. Some moisture must be retained.

After drying, the leaves are piled in a heap for three days. This allows a sweating process to take place which renders the crisp leaf soft and pliable. After sweating, the leaves are dried again in the sun for half an hour or so and then packed. They should still contain a slight amount of moisture. If dried to brittleness, they will lose their distinctive aroma and much of the quality will be destroyed. When dry they should appear olive-green and be pliable, clean, smooth and somewhat glossy. Brownish-green leaves are not nearly as good.

If the sun is not out, drying can be done in an oven, but great care must be taken not to overdry the leaves. Preheat the oven to 200°F, turn off the heat and place a tray of leaves in the oven for 15 minutes. Then remove the tray and turn the leaves. Ones that are adequately dried should be removed. The oven is then reheated and the process repeated until all leaves are properly dried. Never turn on the heat while leaves are in the oven.

PESTS

The pests described here are those which may attack coca plants in Peru. Not all of these will be encountered in other locations. However, one might watch for similar situations anywhere and from these descriptions have some insights into the problem and how to cope with it.

Ulo: This a small butterfly which may attack plants below 4000 feet elevation. During dry spells it deposits its eggs on the plant. When the larvae develop they devour the young and tender leaves. Malthion or a similar systemic insecticide, used as directed long enough before harvesting, will wipe out this pest and do no harm to the product.

Mougna: This insect usually establishes itself in older plantations. It gets into the trunk and causes withering of the plant. Malthion or a similar product should save the plants if this is discovered and treated in time.

Cuqui: This is a species of ant which cuts into the roots, chews up the bark and leaves, and can destroy an entire plantation overnight. Ordinary ants will not do this. The cuqui ants build nests of leaves, twigs and earth, and construct underground water channels to their hills. The best way to get rid of them is to seek out and destroy the anthills.

Taja: This is a fungus which establishes itself on tender or injured twigs, especially if the plant is poorly nourished. If these pre-disposition conditions are avoided, this disease can usually be prevented. Otherwise a systemic fungicide must be resorted to.

Weeds: Any fast-growing weed plants that take nour-
ishment from the soil must be removed. In the Andes
weeding is usually done only (but always) at harvest
time. The weeds which present the greatest problem
to coca plantations are: *Panicum platicaule, P.
scandens, P. decumbens, Pannisetum Peruvianum,
Pteris arichnoidea,* and various *Drimara* species.

Lichens: Various species of *Parmelia* and *Usnea*
lichens, known locally as *lacco,* frequently occur on
the twigs and branches of the coca plant. These are
apparently harmless and certainly useful. Because
these lichens shield the bark from light, they help to
increase the alkaloid yield.

BUYING AND DEALING

Cocaine sold on the underground market in the USA is usually smuggled from South America, where it is obtained for about $6000 a kilo. It is then broken down to ounces, which sell here for $1800–$2000 each. Frequently these ounces are cut with mannite or another standard adulterant. The smaller dealer cuts the coke again and packages it as grams. These are sold for $80–$120 each, depending on the purity. Even when the product is only slightly cut, tremendous profits can be made buying and selling cocaine. If a dealer purchases an ounce (28 grams) for $2000 and adulterates it with 25% of an inexpensive cut, he will have 35 grams to sell. Assuming that the original ounce was pure, the addition of a quarter-ounce of adulterant would make it 80% pure. This is very clean coke by today's standards. Each gram would easily sell for $120. If the original material were not cut, the 28 grams would bring in $3360 — a clear profit of $1360. The 35 grams with the 25% cut would gross $4200, netting $2200 on a $2000 investment. Furthermore, the grams would probably not be full weight. Most dealers would fudge a little on the weight and come up with 40 "grams," which will gross $4800 and net $2800.

These are conservative estimates. Generally, cocaine is cut more severely than this. Gross profits may even triple the investment. Compare these figures with the estimated profits from marijuana sales. $2000 might buy four pounds of decent-quality grass that could sell for $50 per one-ounce lid. After breaking the four pounds down to ounces, the 64 lids would bring in $3200, netting only $1200. Light ounces might raise this figure slightly, but since it is virtually impossible to cut marijuana, the net profit would not exceed $1600. To sell all of the grass, 64 to 72 individual sales would have to be made, in comparison to 35 or 40 coke sales.

STORING COCAINE

Under normal circumstances cocaine will not deteriorate with time. It is quite stable and does not react with any of the known cuts. Moisture can damage the product, and prolonged exposure to sunlight may also cause deterioration. Glass containers are best for storing larger amounts of cocaine. These should be tightly closed. Plastic pill bottles may also be used, but these sometimes crack. Residual cocaine dust will cling to the inside of plastic containers, but this can be rinsed out with a small amount of warmed vodka and imbibed. It is not necessary to refrigerate cocaine for long storage, but exposure to heat may damage it.

TIPS ON BUYING

It is not necessarily so that all or even most cocaine dealers are dishonest. Nevertheless, since it is so easy to cut the product and to fudge on the weight without the customer knowing it, it is almost unfairly tempting for the dealer to cheat a little. These days the righteous dealer may be defined as one who cuts his coke by not more than 20%. Other than the information given in the chapter on testing cocaine in this book, there is little that can be suggested for obtaining relatively pure cocaine. Still, a few general recommendations may be made. First, try to find a dealer whom you know and who can be trusted. Success in doing so will doubtless be the result of much trial and error. Many dealers give out samples from their own stash of uncut cocaine and then sell from their stock of adulterated material. If you are running tests on the product, see that the entire supply is kept before you until the tests are complete and the transaction made. It might be a good idea to keep a copy of this book and perhaps some test tubes and beakers lying about when your dealer visits. He will probably think twice before trying to foist off badly-cut coke on a person who is apparently armed with knowledge and equipment to test the worth of the product.

PACKAGING GRAMS

Grams and half-grams of cocaine are almost always packaged in tiny envelopes (about 1¼ × 2½") folded from a 5½-inch-square sheet of paper, as shown in the

illustrations below. A piece of paper measuring 8½ ×
5½ is obtained by dividing a sheet of typing paper (8½
× 11) in half.

The best material to use for the packaging is ordinary typing paper or 50–70 lb. offset stock; that is,
paper like this book is printed on. Do not use rigid
paper or cover stock. It tends to snap when being
opened and may catapult the contents all over the
place. Some dealers fold their packages from pages of
Playboy, Penthouse, etc., bearing photos of nude mod-
els. This is done to add attractiveness to the package.
It is not a good idea, however. The printing ink comes
off and discolors the cocaine. Although it is not the
customary practice, some dealers put their merchandise in a tape-sealed or heat-sealed plastic coin envelope and place this inside the folded package. The
advantages of doing so include protection against
dampness and less chance of accidental spillage.
When the cocaine is used up, some will cling to the
inside of the coin envelope. The envelope can be cut
open and the residue licked out. Occasionally cocaine
is packaged in aluminum foil. This is not recommended. Foil crinkles easily, forming fissures which
trap the cocaine or make it difficult to get at. Also, the
foil tends to crack, tear or form pinholes, through
which the product may be lost. Many brands of aluminum foil are coated with a wax-like substance. Cocaine
kept in foil can pick up the taste of this coating.

In recent years responsible dealers in the USA have
been putting up various drugs in labeled packages
which state on the outside what the product is and the
weight. When the envelope is partially opened, instructions are found which describe the drug's effects

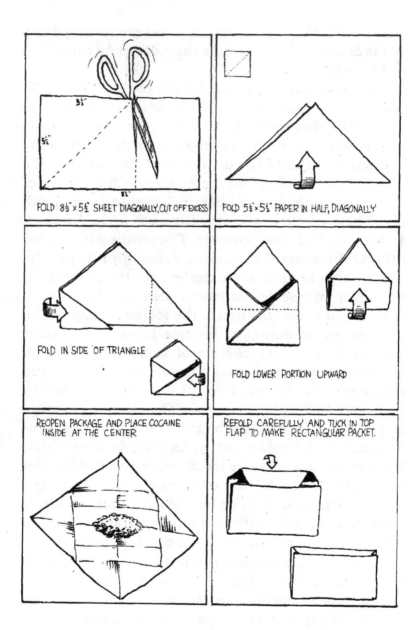

FOLD 8½" × 5½" SHEET DIAGONALLY, CUT OFF EXCESS

FOLD 5½" × 5½" PAPER IN HALF, DIAGONALLY

FOLD IN SIDE OF TRIANGLE

FOLD LOWER PORTION UPWARD

REOPEN PACKAGE AND PLACE COCAINE INSIDE AT THE CENTER

REFOLD CAREFULLY AND TUCK IN TOP FLAP TO MAKE RECTANGULAR PACKET.

and explain how to use and not abuse the product. Below is a label of this sort for cocaine. Copies can be made by any offset printer or on a Xerox machine. The copyright to this design belongs to the Twentieth Century Alchemist. Permission to reproduce it is hereby granted to any supplier of cocaine or individual who wishes to use it for packaging his product. Permission to reproduce the design is not given to any person or company intending to sell empty labeled packages or to offer it as a give-away item or bonus for promotion of commerce. It is not the intention of the author or publisher that this labeled package be filled with cocaine in any country where that product is illegal.

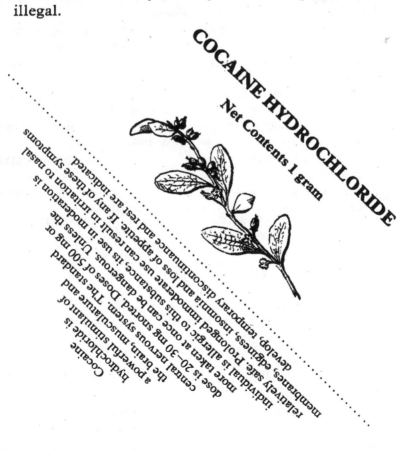